CORRUPTION IN INDIA

Causes, Effects and Reforms

Chitra G. Lele

ATLANTIC

PUBLISHERS & DISTRIBUTORS (P) LTD

ATLANTIC
PUBLISHERS & DISTRIBUTORS (P) LTD
7/22, Ansari Road, Darya Ganj, New Delhi
Tel.: +91-11-4077 5252, 2327 3880
E-mail: orders@atlanticbooks.com
Web: www.atlanticbooks.com

Reprint 2025

Published by Atlantic Publishers & Distributors (P) Ltd.

Printed & bound in India by Atlantic Print Services

Dedicated to

A very sincere and special person,
my Mother, Mrs. Asha Lele

Also Dedicated to the Spirit of Sincerity
And the Heart of Honesty

The illustrations are a product of the imagination of the Author.

They bear no similarity to real people or situations. Any resemblance to real names and situations is purely coincidental and unintentional.

The statistics in the book are taken from the data and research in the public domain. Neither the author nor the publisher assumes any responsibility for the accuracy of these statistics.

Foreword-I

Chitra G. Lele, the young management consultant, peace ambassador and record-setting author's elaborate book on corruption is commendable. As an author she has received letters of commendation for her literary contributions from the Hon'ble President of India; Her Highness Queen Elizabeth II, and other prominent personalities. The book, *Corruption in India: Causes, Effects and Reforms* strives to bring the readers to a level of knowledge and information that may enable them to fight the forces of corruption surrounding them, irrespective of the country that they reside in or operate from. Of course, being aware of the presence of the corruption devil in the system is one thing, but tackling it is completely a different kettle of fish. Many of us crave for eradicating corruption from our lives and systems and listen to, with hope, the sermonizing leaders, but as individuals we are nonplussed because we do not know where to start. And Chitra's book is a good place to start.

This book treats corruption in a manner that a textbook might. It analyzes different dimensions of corruption as well as its latent resides in our ongoing governing and administrating systems. With an added dose of abstraction, of temporal and spatial coverage, the book could be adopted in the studies of social science.

Whether you read the complete book or not, or you read it with cursory interest, you would do well to take a look at the comprehensiveness of the content by referring to the list of chapters. This is a complete mirroring of the issues and content.

While dealing with the role of other countries towards helping India recover from this malady, Chitra has tried to capture the essence of the effort of the international organizations that participate in this activity, the mean and instruments that they use, and the moral and ethical commitment that they all display. Yet, there is this major handicap, that the countries are themselves immersed neck-deep in corruption, and are engaged in eradicating corruption from their own countries as well. It is evident from the experiences of agencies like Interpol, that money laundering, drug trafficking and international organized crime is as much entrenched in the society as the local corruption is.

Corruption may have increased in recent years in different countries, but more of it is the result of information explosion that unravels and unfolds through the media like broadcast, social networks, and the internet in general; something that was missing in the past. So corruption now exists with enhanced presence. I am always intrigued about the instruments and tools that people use to determine the size of corruption in a scam, and further the gains that its avoidance would have delivered to the society. And certainly the figures are mind-boggling to say the least. Chitra has captured all these aspects in a comprehensive manner.

One can expect Chitra to address these questions in her book, "What if corruption was to be switched off from the country, overnight?" "Will the public-private-partnership, or build-operate-transfer model of project funding that is the favorite trend of today's governments, collapse?" "Will the on-going operations in the government machinery come to a standstill?" "Is there an algorithm, a practicable one that can smoothen out the corruption cleansing initiatives?"

If we know about the roots and processes that promote and nourish corruption, and if we have our intentions set morally right we could direct our minds to keep corruption at bay, at least from our personal angle. And Chitra brings out this aspect lucidly in her book.

Mike Rana
Group Captain (Retd.) Indian Air Force,
Keynote Speaker, Software Consultant and
Author of *A Citizen's Manifesto—A Ray of Hope* and
A Wonderful World—Dreams and Reality

Foreword-II

Chitra G. Lele needs no introduction when it comes to nicely converting libraries into 'knowledge' on the subject concerned to present times. I believe she is the youngest author whose books have been placed at our Library of Parliament. She has many more achievements at the global level too, which makes her stand apart when it comes to writing for a cause.

When Chitra first approached me to write a 'Foreword' for her upcoming book on corruption stating that the source of inspiration for her book is the short book, *Chanakya Niti on Corruption* which I authored a few months back. I was quite surprised and intrigued. 'Chanakya Niti on Corruption' was my attempt to highlight one side of the coin in terms of how Chanakya dealt with 'corruption' 300 BCE in India.

Second side of the coin: From 300 BCE to fast forward to 2014. Chitra brings us to present-day India, where corruption has plagued almost every sphere of our life, our society and the very foundation of this nation. *Corruption in India: Causes, Effects and Reforms* is not just about some anti-corruption movement in recent times, or not just against or about a person or ideology, but a well-researched chronology of scams and scandals we have seen post-independence. It gives account of how few lakhs rupees of scams have graduated into few lakhs of crores rupees scams. The book doesn't just stop here; it brings in a unique angle to the problem, which is, how corruption has gradually spread to all the four pillars of democracy. What started by Legislature and Executive hand-in-hand, has spread to Judiciary and Media eventually. The young author doesn't stop there, she continues further, all other sectors where our nation aspires to excel or had natural advantage in, each one by one are getting infected by corruption, e.g. Sports, Arts, History and our Defence forces.

Researching and portraying this deadly evil of corruption is no small feat. However what is more interesting to read further in the book is, the solution part—a way forward for us, as a nation, as an individual and as a responsible human being. This book highlights international forums, societies and venues where the framework for tackling corruption at the global stage is in place. It introduces various laws and organizations in India fighting against corruption, how few individuals refused to standby and watch, and how they gave voice to the pains of the common man suffering under corruption.

I admire the depth and span of the subject covered by Chitra in this book. I hope as a concerned citizen one will not only just read about corruption with facts and figures, but at the end will be able to start focusing on the solution part too.

I congratulate Chitra on her journey as an accomplished author and as a management consultant. This well-researched book will surely be a good read for any concerned citizen of India. A must-have book for personal or public library too!

Dev Dantreliya
Author of *Chanakya Niti on Corruption*,
Telecom Consultant and Researcher

Preface

This is my personal cry against the endemic corruption that surrounds us today. Some people blog about it, others mobilize a movement, some others discuss about it, and I decided to pen down a book on it.

The palette of layers of corruption has become an unwanted part and parcel of a common man's life in India, and so has manifested the ill-administration. The Indian media is overflowing with the stories of scams, administrative failures and high-level cover ups, which have deeply degraded the moral fiber of the society. The book, *Corruption in India: Causes Effects and Reforms* is an attempt to cover the many faces and dimensions of corruption in India as well as those in the world, to provide a handle on the agents of corruption and to present a balanced view of the desired reforms.

The book deals with the major question about how the regulatory colonial administration in the bygone eras, later the post-independence socialist regime and its policies, and then the post-liberalization capitalist regime and its policies paved the way for corruption and built the momentum for it. It also deals with the related questions like:

- how corruption in the public sector has been undermining the efforts directed towards reducing poverty and promoting sustainable growth
- how political and corporate greed are undermining the work and efforts of the sincere factions of the society
- to what extent are governmental and non-governmental factions aware of each other's efforts and the extent

to which they cooperate towards the common goal of curbing corruption

- and many other questions.

For understanding the entire fabric and framework of corruption it was necessary to include subjects like:

- History of corruption in India
- Major scams and scandals in India
- Types of Corruption—Political, Moral, Bureaucratic, Corporate, etc.
- Movements and reforms for curbing corruption
- Dynamics of Global Corruption
- And much more...

The book is divided in four parts, each with its own unique focus. The reader's journey begins with analysis and goes on all the way to reform.

Part 1 covers the foundation topics like history, definitions, types, root causes and the connection between corruption and politics in India.

Part 2 delves into the level and types of corruption in India. The chapters in this part deal with a gamut of topics, right from the dynamics of bureaucratic corruption in India to how to tackle the supply side of corruption in India.

Part 3 covers various anti-corruption aspirations in India. This part details out the information on various measures to combat corruption and reform India's governance; and the heroes and their honest efforts to fight against corruption. The last chapter in this part covers the Indian anti-corruption agenda wherein various aspects and mechanisms like tools for engaging citizens, strengthening of RTI as an instrument for enhancing government transparency, strengthening of political will, virtualization of anti-corruption strategies, focus groups for supporting the citizen voice, participatory performance monitoring, anti-corruption initiatives and their dynamics, etc., are discussed.

Part 4 goes beyond the Indian landscape and provides a cross-country analysis to help us pinpoint options for reforms that have worked in other nations and those that can be applied to the Indian situation as well. This part also deals with the cooperative, cross-sector role played by international cooperation agencies, global networks, conference programs and collaborative solutions in combating corruption both in India and on a global level.

Appendix A provides a snapshot of the resources available for further reading and study. Apart from details of books, papers, essays and website links for further reading, this appendix also shares information about various civil sector initiatives, private bodies and government agencies that you could be a part of to contribute your share of efforts in the fight against corruption.

Appendix B contains information and resources on the corruption studies, indices, diagnostic tools, surveys, expert assessments and reports, which not only give us insights on the corruption scenarios in India, but also deal with various aspects like cross-country analysis, overview of corruption-related problems, strengths and weaknesses of anti-corruption tools worldwide, etc.

The reader of this book is everyone who is affected by corruption and wants to join the bandwagon of anti-corruption, i.e., You. Through this book, I want to provide some food for thought to spark up the intellectual independence within each one of us to think of ways of building a moral values-based, corruption-free India, which in turn will help us to achieve our highest potential without having to face the tall barriers of corruption.

This book should motivate the readers, both individuals and institutions to:

1. Become aware of the different dimensions of corruption in India and across the globe.
2. Analyze corruption scenarios that are directly connected with them and provide concrete inputs towards curbing the same.
3. Trigger constructive, spirited discussions in the classroom and in the academia among the analysts, governance specialists, policymakers, investigative

journalists, social activists, community leaders and heroes of anti-corruption.

4. Explore and recommend what it will take to bring back India on the right path.

All the tools needed to facilitate quick understanding are provided—figures and tables that clarify concepts, spotlight sections, food for thought exercises, illustrations that highlight the realities of corruption in India in an intellectually stimulating manner, questions for reflection, and much more.

I hope that the book will contribute to a better understanding of the various dimensions of corruption in India and across the globe, and to a better and doable agenda against corruption. I hope my book will charge one and all into total anti-corruption action!

Chitra G. Lele

Acknowledgements

The process of writing a book involves the support, encouragement and guidance of many people. I am pleased to acknowledge my sincere thanks to those who have helped me either in a direct or indirect way while writing this book.

First and foremost, my special thanks go to my parents, Mrs. Asha Lele and Mr. G.G. Lele. Whenever my spirits lagged, their constant support and faith helped me to regain my intellectual energy and get on with my writing efforts.

I extend my sincere gratitude to God for being my guide, and helping me along the way in so many mysterious ways.

I am heartily thankful to Mike Rana, whose valuable guidance from the initial to the final stage enabled me to complete the book successfully. Thanks to Mike Sir for taking the time to write the scholarly Foreword I for my book.

I owe my deepest gratitude to Dev Dantreliya for writing the scholarly Foreword II. I tender my heartfelt gratitude to Dev Sir for evincing keen interest in my book.

I would like to express my special gratitude to V. Raghunathan for his kind encouragement. Thanks to Raghunathan Sir for taking the time to write a comprehensive Introduction to the book.

I express my deep appreciation for the known and celebrated heroes and unknown and unsung heroes, who are fighting for all of us against the growing menace of corruption.

Without the comprehensive research studies conducted by several premier research firms and anti-corruption agencies, sharing of vital research findings, valuable actionable insights and up-to-date data would have not been possible. Thanks to these firms and agencies for their relentless efforts in keeping us abreast of the latest developments in the dynamics of corruption, both in India and in the world.

It is due to the unstinted help of various subject matter experts whom I met across the globe that I am able to share so many valuable insights with you all. It is because of these thorough professionals that we get to learn eye-opening facts about the various dimensions of corruption in India and across the world. I am grateful to these experts for their thought-provoking experiences and illuminating discussions.

I want to gratefully acknowledge my readers for committing their valuable time to reading this book.

Finally, words alone cannot express the gratitude I owe to Mr. Harjeet Singh, Publication Co-ordinator of M/s Atlantic Publishers and Distributors (P) Ltd., New Delhi. The valuable feedback and ceaseless cooperation from the Atlantic team are greatly acknowledged.

Chitra G. Lele

Introduction

We are among the most corrupt countries in the world, and we knew it even before Anna Hazare single-handedly brought corruption to the nation's centre stage not long ago. We collectively beat our chests at the depth of its roots in our society. We debate endlessly on its causes, nature and solutions. We decry everyone except ourselves as being corrupt. And yet, it is surprising how little we objectively investigate the various aspects of corruption, including: Why are we so corrupt? What are the different kinds and categories of corruption? How corrupt are the bureaucracy, judiciary and the media? How is the opacity in political funding linked systemically to overall corruption? How much would a powerful Lokpal stem this? Is corruption the result of a collective failure of a corrupt leadership which has a deep vested interest in a corrupt system? Or is it the crony capitalism that is largely to blame? Is the public sector more corrupt or the private sector? What is the best point to start if we wish to stem the free fall to the depths of corruption? How much does the Government exert itself in controlling corruption, as much in itself as outside of it? Are the principles of corporate governance helping the corporate sector control their contribution to the country's corruption? How does corruption interfere with poverty alleviation and other social projects? What is the cost of corruption in our economy? Does it increase the costs of our large projects by 20 per cent or 40 per cent or more?

True, the questions may be overwhelming; but we have seldom had the stomach to ask these questions seriously, leave alone find answers to them. Perhaps that's why scholarly studies of corruption in a country are usually inversely proportional to the degree of corruption in that country; and that's why formal studies in our country are few and far between. Alas, there is something concrete happening on this front through Chitra G.

Lele's comprehensive book on corruption, *Corruption in India: Causes, Effects and Reforms*.

Rather than systematically investigate a problem to find solutions to a problem, we often allow the problem to be lost in a din of discussions, deliberations and debates; or else, find ourselves falling victim to the Vishnu incarnation syndrome. This latter side of our personality as a people came up in a discussion with a friend recently over a casual conversation. Let me explain what I mean by the Vishnu incarnation syndrome. We are told by Lord Krishna, aka, Vishnu, in the Gitopadesha that whenever there is loss of dharma in the world and sin prospers, He, Lord Vishnu, takes it upon himself to be born in one or the other form upon this world to set things right. While Lord Vishnu chose to make nine appearances, we have now got so used to Lord's help that we have started creating many more Vishnu avataras of our own. Before independence, Gandhi was our Vishnu–the one answer to our freedom problem; after independence it was Nehru, the one man to steer India through the difficult years; then it was Indira Gandhi, Rajiv Gandhi, Sonia Gandhi...At the peak of anti-corruption movement, our Vishnu was Anna Hazare. And today, a large part of the nation believes that the current Vishnu is Narendra Modi–who will solve all our problems, now that he has arrived on the scene.

Call it our fatalism, if you will. But we always seem to need a Vishnu to take care of all our problems, while we continue to do precious little to help our own lot. Without a Vishnu, we are lost. We do not even try to identify and isolate a problem. In our psyche, as long as a problem is not recognized, it simply does not exist. And that is also why we never find actual solutions to problems, because we do not recognize the problems in the first place. After all, had there been a problem, there would be a Vishnu to attend to it. But the young author is way ahead of her age; she is not a part of this fatalism. She has taken the reigns in her young hands to start a social transformation and anti-corruption bandwagon.

Is it a problem that our cities are rapidly running out of water? Is it a problem that 67 years after Independence, nearly half our population is still poor, illiterate and malnourished? Is it a problem that our towns and cities do not have sidewalks for people to walk on? Is it a problem that a country of 1.3 billion people does not have a grounded skilling program for its millions of unemployed and unemployable youth? Is it a problem that our government schools simply do not turn out students with even minimal learning levels or life skills? Is it a problem that 60 per cent of our population defecates in the open? Is it a problem that our Railways are the official couriers of faecal matter across the length and breadth of the country? Is it a problem that our cities, towns and villages resemble a giant garbage heap? Is it a problem that our traffic is among the most unruly in the world? Is it a problem that much of it is because of corruption? Is it a problem that we are among the most corrupt people in the world? True, each of these problems needs a Vishnu to solve. But how concerned are we about these problems, beyond the beating of our chests, that is? How deep do we delve in the understanding of the root cause of many of these problems?

And this is the gap that Chitra Lele overcomes in her splendid book on corruption in India. She is neither an economist nor an anti-corruption activist. She is a young peace ambassador, author and management consultant, but deep down, at the core, she is an enlightened citizen with a scientific temper. In this book, she takes a comprehensive look at corruption in India. When did it start? How? What have been the major contributory factors to our corruption? How does corruption across different spheres of the state interact? What have been the major scams and scandals? What have been the major movements against it? What is the global dynamics of corruption? What are the international drivers, if any? These and many more questions have been answered by Chitra painstakingly to set forth the anatomy of corruption in India in its proper perspective.

But Chitra does not stop there. She provides many insights that, if taken seriously, could provide useful measures to curb many aspects of corruption in the country. She advises triggering constructive and spirited discussions in school classrooms, among policy analysts, governance specialists, investigative journalists, community leaders, social activists and heroes of anti-corruption, so that corruption as our common enemy is imprinted into our very souls.

Corruption is a difficult subject to handle. The writer is often seen, even if unfairly, as being 'holier than thou'. The subject also suffers from issue-fatigue, in the sense that very mention of corruption creates a reaction like, 'Oh, not the same old topic of corruption again!' What is more, almost everyone, his aunt and her cat has their own opinion on corruption, as also its solution. Yes, if Vishnu himself (Anna Hazare), were to write on corruption, some of us may take it seriously, issue fatigue or not. But a young author? Well, that's what the spirit of this young author and her book is all about. If you think corruption is a problem, Chitra's book is a definite read.

V. Raghunathan
Best-selling Author of The Corruption Conundrum
And Other Paradoxes And Dilemmas (Penguin 2010),
Don't Sprint The Marathon (Harper Collins 2010) and
Games Indians Play (Penguin 2006),
Academic and CEO of GMR Varalakshmi Foundation

Contents

PART 3
The Indian Anti-Corruption Aspirations—Where We Need To Be

List of Tables, Figures and Illustrations

PART 1

Corruption in India—Where We Have Come From

1

Corruption in India—The Basics

Right from the definition of corruption to the various types of corruption and from a not so humble beginning to its current rampant status, corruption in India has built up quite a history for itself.

In this chapter, we take a look at the long history of corruption and its many forms. The criminalization of India from Independence to this very day is discussed in here. India tops the list for black money in the entire world with almost US$1456 billion, a figure about 13 times larger than the nation's debt.

Corruption in the Indian society has prevailed from time immemorial in one form or the other. Earlier, Indian corruption was not much talked of in the world as we were a closed economy. It is only from the 1990s that we have created a name for ourselves in global corruption dynamics. This new face of corruption is dealt with in this chapter.

How the regulatory colonial administration in the bygone eras and the post-independence socialist regime and its policies paved the way for corruption and built the momentum for it, right from the days of the Licence Raj to the most recent 2G Spectrum scam is highlighted in this chapter. The most significant growth in the parallel economy occurred during and after the 1960s—here we will study how a new brand of governance and leadership used new factors like caste, religion, vote banks, artificial scarcity and private lobbies to further their interests.

In other words, this chapter traces the history of corruption in India and explores all aspects of this pervasive phenomenon.

1.1 History—From Licence Raj to Capture Economy

Though there is huge hue and cry against corruption in India in recent times, India's history of corruption is a long running and a deep rooted one. Corruption is universal. India completed 67 years of independence in the year 2014, but her dream of being free from the clutches of corruption is yet to be realized.

Right from the pre-liberalization days to the current times of 'capture economy' (in capture economy, powerful individuals run the government, economy and society; everything else is undermined), corruption has increased its web to engulf every nook and corner of India. In our daily routines, most of us have been a victim of corruption or have had first-hand experiences of paying bribes or have been a witness to acts of corruption, either directly or indirectly.

During India's very first General Election (1951-52), bouts of corruption occurred. In 1952, following its first General Election, India became the world's largest democracy. But its political system still follows the structure of power inherited from the British Raj; hence corruption in modern-day India is no different as the parliamentary form of government still follows the principles of dynastic politics, except now we are exploited by our own Indian rulers.

The history of corruption in post-Independence India starts with the Jeep scandal in 1948. This scandal is related to purchase of jeeps for the Indian Army. Indian Government had placed an order for 2,000 jeeps with a London-based firm that had false credentials. While most of the money was paid up front, but just 155 jeeps were delivered. Right from the 1950s all the way till the 1980s, India followed socialist policies of protectionism and regulations. Corruption in this time period was limited to the politicians, elite class and bureaucrats. Then came the Capitalist era where corruption became more pervasive and widespread; it went all the way down to the roots. Thereafter, the scale of corruption expanded all the more with the nexus of politicians, bureaucrats, businessmen and criminals running a parallel government; the elected government has become a mere rubber stamp. The criminalization of politics has sort of made the political leaders the leaders of criminal gangs as they provide state protection to the criminal activities thereby leading to a never-ending stream of illicit financial flows. These illicit financial flows are a product of corrupt activities like bribery, tax evasion, kickbacks and criminal activities. At the same time, criminals have now entered the arena of politics—they are a part of the government machinery and they openly participate in public life without the fear of being apprehended.

The earlier commitment to socialism led to "Licence/Permit Raj," whereas the New Economic Policy since 1990 led to the rise of "Capture Economy/Mafia Raj." The modus operandi of corruption has changed but the impact is still the same, rather much more. Outwardly, it may seem that the days of "Licence Raj" are supposedly over two decades ago, but they do dwell in some form or the other even today. During the Licence Raj, corrupt practices like a licence-permit regime, illegitimate proceeds or scarcity of basic commodities were practiced to make more money. Now, these terms are replaced with modern-day counterparts of globalization, liberalization, knowledge economy and so on and so forth. These modern-day counterparts have in fact accelerated the transfer of illicit money abroad, thus putting Indian corruption on the global corruption map.

On the one hand, over the years, India has risen from the depths of economic depression to the heights of being a potential superpower (but sadly), on the other hand, all this progress comes at a heavy price—an underground economy, a capture state and a subdued mind state of the common man. This price deteriorates all aspects, i.e. each and every household, each and every neighborhood, and each and every organization, in other words, the whole society.

1.1.1 *Definition of Corruption—Wider Context*

What is corruption? There is no universal definition of corruption. Although each and every definition has different nuances, they do not differ in substance. Corruption carries different meanings for different contexts and cultures. In common parlance, corruption is the ways or practices in which a few people manage to get rich and secure power at the expense of society as a whole. The origin of the word is from the Latin corruptus (spoiled) and corrumpere (to ruin; to break into pieces). A comprehensive definition is given by Carl Friedrich—corruption "is a kind of behavior which deviates from the norm actually prevalent or believed to prevail in a given context.... It is deviant behavior associated with a particular motivation, namely that of private gain at public expense.... Such private gain may be monetary one, and in the minds of the general public it usually is, but it may take other forms."

Corruption breeds corruption—"corruption may corrupt," as stated by Andvig and Moene (1990).

There are three main aspects to address before declaring a particular scenario as a scenario of corruption:

A. Transparency

B. Accountability

C. Reciprocity

The following questions help you to understand these three main aspects.

A. **Transparency:** Do you mind if others know or the press reports on what you do?

B. **Accountability:** Do you report your actions to others without fear and with full ownership of the consequences?

C. **Reciprocity:** Would you feel agitated, angry, upset or hurt if others did the same thing?

Spotlight

You live in a society where everybody indulges in corrupt behaviors and practices. Do you choose to indulge in the same? The answers to the above questions are in fact the framework for ethical behaviors. In other words, corruption is of values and ethics and not of the individuals or systems; corruption is the deviation from moral, social, economic, corporate and political norms of ethical behavior.

Do you consider giving money for getting a business permit as corruption? Do you believe giving money to a traffic policeman to avoid speeding tickets as corruption? All these scenarios and many more constitute corruption.

The working definition of corruption put forth by the World Bank is "the abuse of public power for private benefit." The World Bank defines corruption in terms of corrupt, fraudulent, collusive, coercive, obstructive practices.

According to BusinessDictionary.com corruption is "wrongdoing on the part of an authority or powerful party through means that are illegitimate, immoral, or incompatible with ethical standards. Corruption often results from patronage and is associated with bribery."

Another definition for corruption as defined by Transparency International is "the misuse of entrusted power for private gain." This definition is applicable to all types of corruption in India—individual, social, corporate, bureaucratic and political.

Joseph Nye in his article titled "Corruption and Political Development: A Cost-Benefit Analysis", *American Political Science Review*, Vol. 61, No. 2, June 1967, defines corruption as a behavior which deviates from the normal duties of a public role because of private-regarding (family, close private clique), pecuniary or status gain, or violates rules against the exercise of certain types private-regarding influence. This includes such behavior as bribery (use of reward to pervert the judgment of a person in a position of trust); nepotism (bestowal of patronage by reason of ascriptive relationship rather than merit); and misappropriation (illegal appropriation of public resources for private-regarding uses).

In his foreword to the 2004 UN Convention against Corruption, Kofi Annan, the (then) Secretary General to the United Nations defines corruption in the following words: "Corruption is an insidious plague that has a wide range of corrosive effects on societies. It undermines democracy and the rule of law, leads to violations of human rights, distorts markets, erodes the quality of life and allows organized crime, terrorism and other threats to human security to flourish."

Let me add another perspective—corruption in various fields will result in corrupt behavior for different types of gains.

In politics, it is done for political power, status and wealth. The gains may be direct or indirect and they can be achieved through an individual or an organization or a group.

The actors involved in the corruption process follow the principle-agent (PA) model. There are two parties involved in the process—one who receives the inducement or bribe and the other who gives the same.

From the morality perspective, corruption is something that is morally unacceptable.

From the above definitions, we can conclude the following key points about corruption in India:

A. Corruption breeds corruption.
B. Corruption is the subversion of public welfare, public resources, democratic processes and constitutional laws for private good, partisan goals or particularistic gain.
C. Corruption is the product of a system, be it political, corporate, economic or social.
D. A corrupt nation, government and society stop valuing honesty and lack moral principles.
E. Corruption is the abuse of office and power and consequently the people of a nation.
F. Corruption takes on many disguises—graft, misappropriation of public resources, extortion, bribery, nepotism, patronage, embezzlement, etc.

G. Different types of corrupt behaviors and practices result in different types of gains.

1.2 Reasons for Growth—Stimulating Factors

Individual factors like the lack of accountability, ineffective implementation of laws and bad governance do contribute their share towards corruption, but the greatest factor is the nexus between politicians, corporates, bureaucrats and criminals. This nexus is the most dangerous and covert level of corruption.

Let us have a look at how these factors have increased corruption in India.

A. Corrupt political leaders make the spread of corrupt practices at lower levels relatively easy.

B. Social attitude—the tolerance and leniency shown by society towards corruption is yet another major reason.

C. Rampant bureaucracy is the most fertile ground which breeds corruption. Administrative positions and public offices are given the absolute authority and power to carry out their duties and responsibilities, which essentially means that they have ample opportunity to indulge in corrupt practices. The unclear and redundant procedures and the lack of requisite information about their rights, makes the citizens of India more exposed to discretionary exploitation and bureaucratic red tape (bureaucratic red tape refers to excessive regulations and time-consuming procedures that are required to be followed to gain bureaucratic approval).

D. Democratic pluralism—the multi-party system is a huge source of corruption; hence fraudulent leaders and unstable government. Each and every political party spends (wastes) millions of rupees on their election campaigns, vote-bank politics, false media reporting, etc. More the number of parties, higher the level of corruption. In fact, the ingredients of democratic pluralism, liberal economic conditions and capitalism make a perfect recipe for corruption in modern India.

E. The complexity of laws and procedures—this complexity increases the magnitude of corruption.

F. The lack of proper accountability and reporting mechanism combined with a high degree of discretionary powers results in a poor legal framework and no political will to combat corruption.

G. Post-independence, India has witnessed more and more illegal financial flows. The report by Global Financial Integrity (GFI is non-profit, research and advocacy organization aimed at curbing illicit financial flows and enhancing global development and security) found that the higher rates of economic growth since economic reform started in 1991 led to a deterioration of income distribution, which led to more illicit flows in the form of bribery, tax evasion, etc., from India.

H. Absence of laws to protect the whistleblowers—the proposed legislation of "Public Interest Disclosure and Protection to Persons Making the Disclosure Bill, 2010" authorizes the Central Vigilance Commission (CVC) (CVC is an apex body set up by the Government of India to deal with corruption in Central Government institutions and public administration and also to advise various authorities in Central Government organizations in planning, executing, reviewing and reforming their vigilance work) to punish those who disclose a whistleblower's identity. However, this is insufficient and stricter norms should be implemented to protect the whistleblowers who disclose information of government and private companies' acts of corruption and wrongdoings.

I. Stress is laid on the wrong aspects of life like monetary progress and cut-throat competition, both in the academic setup and home environment. Moral and spiritual values are not given utmost importance in both educational systems and at home, which is highly responsible for the deterioration of the individuals, and eventually of the society. It is sad to note that the society and the upbringing level of individuals are deteriorating day by day, and are being compromised for short-cut success, transitory progress and get-rich-quick attitude.

J. Financing the political parties and elections is a common aspect of the Indian democracy. Corruption in elections leads to a lop-sided representation. This financing is mainly done by big business houses, so naturally the elected representatives are bound to use their powers for the benefit of these business houses, even if they have to go against the common man's interests. For example, the ruling party granting contracts that are non-environment friendly to those who sponsored its election funds. Another interlinked reason for corruption is that there are currently no regulations that require parties or candidates to disclose the donations they receive.

K. Collusion between corrupt taxpayers and corrupt tax officials breeds corruption. This collusion can also tempt honest taxpayers to evade taxes. High tax rates deter compliance and therefore lead to an increase in corruption. Corrupt tax officials and taxpayers weaken the honesty and will of honest officials and taxpayers.

1.3 Scams and Scandals—From Jeeps to 2G Spectrum

Corruption scams, swindles or scandals—all mean one thing—disgrace to a nation. The following list is but a mere drop of the deep ocean of corruption in India; the cauldron of corruption is constantly boiling to the brim with corruption scams. If we were to detail out each and every scam, it would take several volumes to do so. Undoubtedly, there is one common factor running through the long list of corruption scams—the truth, which the sincere taxpayer has every right to know but it never ever reaches him; they both are the biggest victim.

Illustration 1.1: The Cauldron of Corruption

Let us take a quick scan of some of the major scams that occurred on the Indian horizon from 1948 till recent times.

A. Jeep Purchase (1948)—by distorting regulations and bypassing protocols, a deal worth ₹ 80 lakh rupees for jeeps for the Indian Army in Kashmir was signed with a foreign firm. The case for this scam was closed in 1955, despite the demand of the opposition for judicial inquiry.

B. Mundhra scandal (1957)—the first big financial scandal of free India in the 1950s. It involved the sale of fictitious shares to the insurance giant, Life Insurance Corporation. The investment was done under governmental pressure and in the process LIC lost most of the money.

C. Bofors Payoff (1987)—a major scandal of the 1980s. Here several prominent politicians, high profile businessmen and brokers were accused of receiving massive kickbacks from Bofors AB for winning a bid to supply India's 155 mm field howitzer. A well-thought out cover-up operation was mounted by the accused in order to displace the inquiry into the allegations of commission payments. Most of the accused have died of old age whereas the investigation is still going on. The sheer mismanagement of public resources involved in this scam is shocking as the amount of money spent on the investigation is much higher than the amount involved in alleged kickbacks, payoffs and commission payments. For more than two decades, this scam has been in the news circuit.

D. Securities scam (1992)—it involved misappropriation of funds to the tune of over ₹ 3500 crores. The stock market and money market were in doldrums, and there was a prolonged closure of the stock exchanges. There was deep panic among brokers and investors. The share market faced a massive loss to the tune of ₹ 100,000 crores.

E. And many more...

India was hit by a series of scams since independence, but in the year of 2010 India has been rocked by a series of big corruption scandals. India is known for its traditions and cultural heritage, but the recent series of scams involving unimaginably large amounts of money has tarnished its image on the international front. The scams in India have increased in scope, scale and audacity over the years, in a rapid manner. According to the research figures, the total amount of money involved in various scams over the last 10-15 years is estimated to be over a mind-boggling ₹ 80 trillion. In last 10-15 years, some of the top corruption scams that have grabbed headlines and exposed high profile people are as follows:

A. Hawala Scam (1996)—Hawala is the biggest ever scandal in the world which involved over 115 top politicians and bureaucrats of the country. It involved the alleged payments that politicians received from hawala brokers. Due to the lack of hard evidence, everyone was let off. Hawala is a system of underground banking purely based on trust whereby money can be made available internationally without actually moving it or leaving a record of transactions.

B. Fodder Scam (1996)—a corruption scandal that involved the alleged embezzlement of about 950 crores from the State Government Treasury of the eastern Indian state of Bihar. Ministers, corporates and bureaucrats colluded to bill the state treasury over ₹ 950 crores to provide medicines, animal husbandry equipment and feed for "vast herds of fictitious livestock."

C. Tehelka Sting (2001)—through its sting operation 'Operation Westend,' Tehelka exposed the corruption underlying India's large defence contracts. This operation was a major milestone in investigative journalism.

D. Scorpene Submarine deal (2005)—secret Navy documents were sold to the makers of the Scorpene submarine, Thales, through various middlemen from the Navy. ₹ 500 crores were alleged to have been paid to government decision makers by Thales.

E. Stamp paper scam (2006)—this multi-crore scam involved complex and expansive counterfeiting of stamp paper, and it had spread its web of operations across 12 states. It involved selling of fake stamp papers to bulk purchasers like insurance companies, stock market players and banks. The scam involved the sale of not only counterfeit stamp paper but also related items such as revenue stamps, foreign bills, judicial court fee stamps, broker notes, etc.

F. Satyam Computers scam (2009)—the biggest fraud in the Indian corporate world involving approximately 70 billion Indian rupees. In this scam, the company's financial records had been fudged and manipulated and profit levels were falsely inflated for the last several years. Approximately 1.5 billion US dollars of the company's past funds were "non-existent." It is dubbed as "India's Enron."

G. 2G Spectrum (2010)—by far the biggest political scam in modern Indian history. Here the telecom bandwidth was being grossly undervalued and offered to a chosen few with vested interests, resulting in a huge loss amounting to a humongous figure of $40 billion. Dubious 2G licenses were distributed at throw-away prices that were pegged at 2001 prices. The groups involved in this scam—politicians and bureaucrats who had the authority to sell the licenses, media professional who liaised between the politicians and corporations, and corporations who were buying the frequency allocation licenses.

H. Commonwealth Games (2010)—right from the infrastructure projects to medical equipment, everything was overrated, and there were huge misappropriations, over-inflated prices and discrepancies in tenders. The whole project was shrouded in a blanket of allegations—right from environmental concerns to racism. This ₹ 8000 crore scam was unearthed by the Comptroller and Auditor General of India even before the conduct of the games. The Central Bureau of Investigation and India's anti-corruption watchdog have identified more than 16 projects with possible irregularities.

I. Adarsh Housing Society (2010)—the Adarsh Society is a cooperative society in the city of Mumbai; it was reserved for the war widows and veterans of the Kargil War. Right from plot procurement and environmental concerns to records and clearance given to ineligible members, everything was found to be highly suspicious. This project violated the Indian environment ministry rules. The Comptroller and Audit General of India stated it was a classic example of the "fence eating the farm", or a case of the protector taking away what must be protected. This scam is a shameful case of how leading politicians, high-ranking military officials and influential bureaucrats colluded not for a common noble cause, but for selfish personal interests.

J. IPL (Indian Premier League) (2010) scam—on the one hand, IPL has taken cricket to a new level altogether, and on the other hand, it has done more damage to the image of cricket than one can imagine due to the heavy embezzlement involved in the bidding process of various franchisees. 2010 was definitely the year of shocking scams.

K. Mining scams—Right from the illegal mining in Uttarakhand in Ganga river riverbed for stones and sand for construction work to the illegal iron ore mining and export scam in Karnataka, there was a series of mining scams that rocked the nation. These scams exemplify the strong nexus that exists between politicians, bureaucrats and mining barons. In places like Bellary, it is said that the entire government machinery is paid by the mining barons.

L. And the list goes on...

1.4 Types—From Petty to Political

For most people in India, when they hear the term corruption, bribery is the first word that comes to their mind. But there is more to it than merely offering money or 'bakshish.' Bribery is just one type of corruption. There are several types, scales and levels of corruption that attribute to 'deviant' behaviors. On the one end of the spectrum, there is political corruption like a defence minister receiving kickbacks for passing an arms deals, and on the other end, corruption could take on a petty form like paying bribe for getting away with breaking traffic rules or graft paid to a junior civil servant for expediting a driver's license. The Central Vigilance Commission has recognized as many as 33 different modes of corruption. Let us discuss the main types:

A. Political corruption—refers to the abuse of legislated political powers by government officials to amass private wealth and to maintain their hold on power through illegal means.

   As politicians enjoy a lot of privileges associated with their high office, they sideline policy-making and direction (which is their true portfolio) and get busy in making money—which is the primary occupation of a large number of them now.

   Political corruption is all about private gain and party gain and also about power preservation.

   Political corruption reduces accountability and transparency. It undermines the democratic setup and the constitution.

B. Bureaucratic corruption—this is corruption happening at the implementation end of politics. Everyone is aware that bureaucrats demand huge under-the-table payoffs to carry out their duties. Bureaucrats adopt several measures for increasing their gains, right from lobbying politicians to demanding side payments to provide an export license.

   This type of corruption and opportunistic behavior not only takes the general public for a ride, but also distorts regulations and constitutional rules.

   Bureaucrats can also form interest groups to put pressure on the political system in order to gain more wealth from national resources. In such cases of corruption, the civil servants' total extra compensation is dependent on his/her skills to exploit the various sources. Bureaucracy is the place where the gullible public meets the cunning public officials and the public gets duped day in and day out for all that they rightfully deserve.

   Bureaucrats have been bestowed with discretionary powers, which give them the advantage of interpreting, altering and applying rules as they wish. As they are vested with powers to bend the rules as per their convenience, naturally they are bound to indulge in corrupt behaviors.

C. Judicial corruption—the huge backlog of pending cases testifies for the slow and inefficient functioning of the judiciary. Often to speed up the process, people have to pay bribes. This expensive system is out of the common man's reach. The influential (which most of the times are the criminals) twist and distort judicial provisions and laws in their favor by paying bribes to judges/jury or by manipulating witnesses in order to get a judgment in their favor. Bribes and influences can be exerted also to speed up and slow down cases, fabricate or omit evidence, and fudge sentences. The law-breakers have become the law-makers today.

   Bribery and influence from political parties and businesses are the two main types of judicial corruption.

   A corrupt judicial system also means that the mechanisms, agencies and laws designed to curb corruption are being compromised.

D. Corporate corruption—it encompasses cases that range from white-collar crime to organized crime. Corporate corruption in India can easily be classified into two subtypes: corruption by PSUs (public sector units) and that by the private sector.

   Another classification for corporate corruption includes three types—organized, white-collar and state-corporate. Organized corruption involves setting up of corporations by criminals to channelize their criminal activities. White-collar corruption involves the individuals working in an organization, who represent the interests of their organization. State-corporate corruption emerges from the nexus that exists between the state and corporations.

E. Another classification includes two types of corruption—organized and chaotic corruption.

Organized corruption and crime are connected with words like mafia, gangs and crime syndicates. In organized corruption, there are clear-cut guidelines for all the involved parties in terms of whom to pay, how much to pay and the guarantee that the payment made will fulfill the desired request/favor, whereas in the case of chaotic corruption, there is a lot of confusion as there is nothing predetermined, for example, a business enterprise may have to pay several times to several agents to acquire a permit, and yet there is no guarantee that even after several payments made, the required permit will be granted; there is no coordination and tracking at all. Buying protection from the state is a necessary condition for the growth of organized corruption.

F. A further classification is broader in nature—public and private. Public corruption can be committed by anyone appointed, elected or hired on the national, state or local level. For example, a pliant judge, an insincere law enforcement officer, etc. Private corruption refers to the corruption carried out by individuals, organizations and companies in the private sector, which leads to unfair competition and distorts markets.

G. High-level, low-level and petty corruption—corruption in the political, judicial, bureaucratic or corporate areas is considered as high-level corruption, whereas corruption involving civil servants who indulge in corrupt activities because of low salaries is labeled as low-level corruption. Petty corruption typically involves smaller sums and junior officials, for example, bribing officials for evasion of income tax.

H. The flow of money or other resources also determines the type of corruption. If the flow is from the society to the state then it is called extractive corruption or corruption from above, and when it is in the reverse direction, from the state to the society, it is referred to as redistributive corruption or corruption from below.

I. A further distinction can be made between individual corruption and organizational or institutional corruption.

> **A Word of Caution**
>
> No type or level of corruption is better or worse than another.

Table 1.1: Types of Corruption

Political	**Judicial**	**Corporate**
Manipulation of elections and vote-buying	Influence and pressure from businesses	Tax evasions
Nepotism and patronage	Influence and pressure from political parties	Trademark infringements
Commissions and fees taken from private sector businesses	Blocking the reports of criminal activities	Tweaking the processes for approval and licensing
Use of public money for political campaigns	Bribery	Misrepresentation in financial statements
Embezzlement	Repeated violations of due processes	Commercial bribery
Bribery	Abuse of human rights	Misappropriation of funds
Buying media and civil society	Delaying justice	Manipulation in the stock market
Bureaucratic	**Organized**	
Arbitrary exercise of power	Racketeering	
Irregularities in the granting of import and export licences	Money laundering	
Nepotism	Collusion between criminal groups, politicians and public officials	
Bribery	Extortion	

We will discuss each of the types of corruption in more detail as we proceed further. Several studies reveal that all these types and levels of corruption tend to coexist and reinforce each other.

1.5 Questions for Reflection

A. What are the factors you would take into account in determining whether a particular scenario is a case of corruption or not?

B. What are the main problems of corruption in your country?

C. What is your personal definition of corruption?

D. Is chaotic corruption more harmful than organized corruption?

E. Which areas (whether in private or public sector) you consider as particularly vulnerable to corruption?

F. How does organized crime influence the spread of corrupt practices in a country?

G. Why should advanced nations be concerned about corruption in poor nations?

2

Roots in India–Deep, But can be Uprooted, Considerably

Corruption is no longer confined to the political sphere and the administrative apparatus; it is not just a political problem anymore. It is intertwined with the economy and the society as well. It cuts across regions, faiths and ethnicities. This chapter provides a systematic overview of different theories on the causes of corruption—historical roots and the contemporary causes like globalization. Globalization poses both opportunities and challenges to reforms in developing countries—this chapter describes the role of globalization in the dynamics of modern-day corruption. The World Bank has identified corruption as one of the single largest impediment to social and economic progress.

This chapter discusses the root causes of corruption as an economic problem, societal problem and political problem. The causes of corruption must first be correctly diagnosed so that the civic society, political leaders, anti-corruption organizations, business entities, social activists, community leaders and heroes of anti-corruption projects can take appropriate action to minimize these causes.

For political corruption, we study the various causes like the lack of accountability, ineffective punitive and combative measures, etc. For societal degeneration, we discuss the existence of a social environment that is conducive to corrupt practices, social norms and religious traditions that lay stress on gift-giving (both in cash and in kind), etc. For economic corruption, the relationship dynamics between corporate governance, business houses and corruption are explained.

Pertinent factors like inadequate reforms of political representation, policy design and implementation loopholes, the Indian bureaucracy today, gaps in leadership, lack of knowledge in the people, etc., are addressed to establish the causal chain between politics, society and economy.

For the consequences and measures for curbing the various types of corruption, separate chapters are included in the book.

2.1 Root Causes—The Sources of Corruption

Corruption has permeated each and every aspect of India and has engulfed the whole society. According to the findings of the Transparency International's Global Corruption Barometer Survey 2010, 74 percent Indians believed that the level of corruption has increased during the last three years, compared with the world average of 56 percent and Asia-Pacific average of 47 percent.

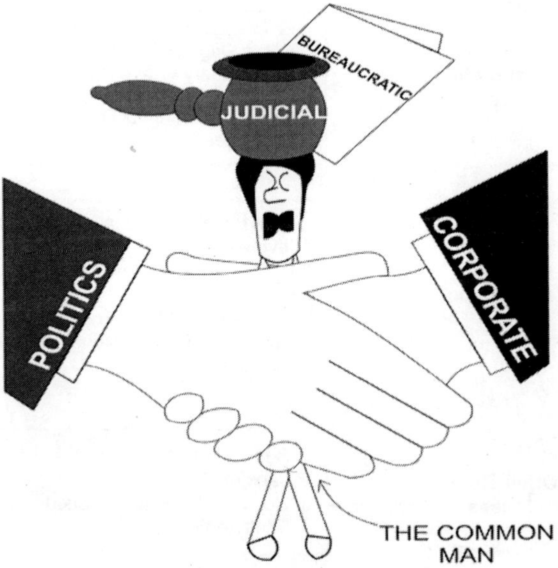

Illustration 2.1: The Common Man is Crushed by the Root Causes

No matter how we categorize corruption, understanding the causes of corruption is very crucial for developing well-thought-out strategies for dealing with the same. These causes come from various sources, both in monetary and human form. Where do the funds allocated for the public welfare disappear?—Not into thin air, but into thick pockets of the corrupt elements of society.

It is hard to decide which are the causes and which are the effects. Is the society or government responsible for corruption? Both are responsible, because the causes or sources of corruption have a degenerative effect on the welfare of the whole society. It is essential to understand the various root causes that result in legally and socially prohibited favors, only then we as individuals and as a whole society can take concrete steps to combat corruption.

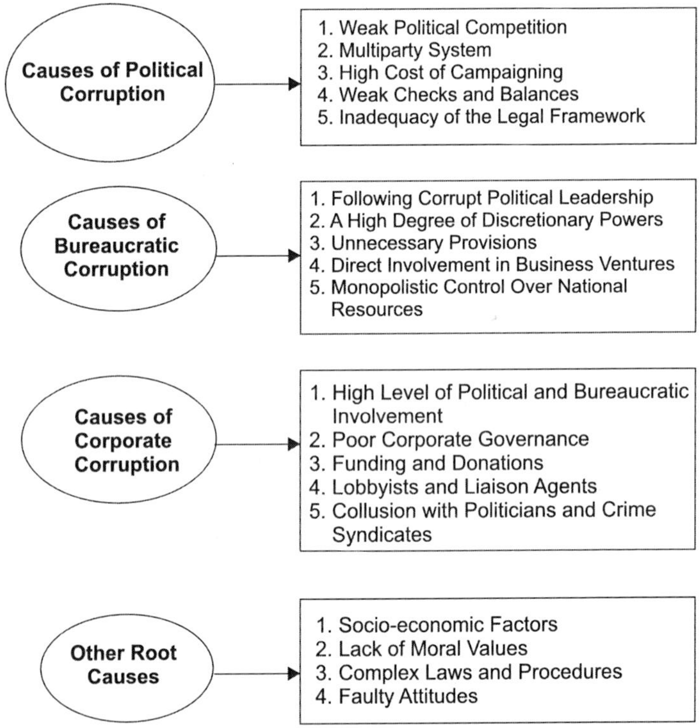

Figure 2.1: Causes of Corruption

Corruption is like diabetes—it cannot be rooted out completely, but it can surely be curbed and contained, considerably.

> **Spotlight**
>
> Greed is the main cause responsible for all types of corruption—whether a high-ranking leader or a top-notch company executive or a clerk in the local government, all their actions and concentration are bent on corruption.
>
> The key to curbing corruption is disabling its causes.

2.1.1 *Eye-Opening Scams—The Thieves of Public Welfare*

The scams and their scale definitely stand out in the crowd, but for all the wrong reasons. Just imagine if all this scam money is fed back into the society for good purposes—the welfare and progress of the common man and the sincere taxpayers—because this is where all the swindled resources rightfully belong to.

Table 2.1: The Scale of Corruption in India

Scam and Year	Scale of Money	Scam Money Put to Good Uses
Jeep Purchase, 1948	80 lakhs	Primary schools
BHU Funds, 1956	50 lakhs	Medical facilities for the needy like infant polio vaccines
Mundhra Scandal, 1957	1.25 crores	
Teja Loans, 1960	22 crores	Setting up productivity-enhancing infrastructure in terms of employment generation, agricultural research and extension, rural development, etc.
Bofors, 1987	65 crores	
Securities Scam, 1992	5000 crores	
Sugar Import, 1994	650 crores	Computer education
Stock Market Scam, 2001	1,15,000 crores	Mid-day meals
2G Spectrum, 2010	1,76,000 crores	Public utilities like water supply, bridges, parks, dams, sewage, hospitals, electricity generation, etc.

The causes of corruption are the source and the end-result of corruption—it is there for you all to see in Table 2.1. To realize the good aspect, i.e. the third column in the table, we first need to understand the root causes in order to deal with them through effective anti-corruption measures.

According to a study (as shown in Table 2.2) released in the *Times of India*, a leading Indian English-language daily newspaper, 98 percent of the respondents believed that the politicians are corrupt and 38 percent believed that ordinary people are corrupt.

Table 2.2: People's Perception

Occupation	% believing
Politicians	98
Police	97
Government Servants	88
Lawyers	80
Businessmen	76
Bank officials	69
Judges	66
Journalists	55
Teachers	43
Ordinary people	38

Source: MODE poll, "Corruption All-Pervasive: Survey", *Times of India* (January 14, 1995), p. 1.

2.2 Causes of Political Corruption—The Forerunner

Indian politics is based on democracy and India's democracy is the largest in the world. A multiparty system denotes more parties—a large government. Naturally, a large government is bound to generate more corruption. The current state of politics exemplifies the proverb of "Power tends to corrupt, and absolute power corrupts absolutely." At one point in time more than 20 percent of the members of the Lok Sabha have had criminal cases pending against them.

The strong nexus between politicians, criminal elements, bureaucratic officials and business houses has made organized crime and corruption a pervasive reality. Politicians use this alliance to build a network of money power and muscle power, which is used by them during elections for garnering votes through fear or threat, and for other purposes like use of criminal violence to do away with competition and for personal gains. And in return, politicians promise the criminals cabinet posts and legal delays in their cases.

Criminal gangs and syndicates need legitimate state structures to sustain and expand their activities. The political setup is the perfect setup for criminals as it facilitates the circulation of illicit goods and money laundering. And all this is done for huge payoffs in return.

Spotlight

Academic literature states that corruption tends to increase in a period of rapid growth as new sources of wealth and power become available, and this is what exactly happened in the period of post-liberalization (since 1991).

Weak political competition and the lack of a cogent ideology is yet another reason for rampant political corruption. As political leaders experience a relatively low risk of replacement, they continue with their corrupt acts audaciously in a way that constitutes a breach of law or social norms.

Research has proved that the very thought of having the authority or the ability and power to be corrupt is a major cause of corruption. This is further fueled by the fact that there is a decline in ethics and morals at all levels of the society, which in a way, gives the politicians a boost. Moreover, the common man fears reporting illegal activities of the politicians as he knows that even the law of the land is in their pockets.

The cost of campaigning and winning elections is beyond imagination. This is one of the major reasons behind the acts of political corruption.

The cultural context, too, is one major cause that made political corruption with the passage of time an accepted tradition; the culture of a complacent attitude shown by the people of India has become conducive for political corruption. The cultural norms also emphasize and prefer the practice of gift-giving over the rule of the law.

Corporate money is an entrance gate for political corruption. Each and every party needs more money to ensure a level playing field. For doing so, party funds are not sufficient and this is where funding, donations and contributions from corporate houses step in. This in turn gives the business houses the privilege to exert influence on the parties and those that are elected. To fulfill partisan goals and return favors, parties have to award contracts, concessions and other opportunities to those who sponsored the political parties and their elections.

The extent of corruption in the field of politics is much more than the other areas—in all aspects: amount of money, number of citizens affected, number of officials involved, and number of institutions and agencies involved. There are very loosely defined anti-corruption regulations, and weak checks and balances to stop such a huge scale of corruption. Again this is an incentive in itself for the politicians to go rampant on their corruption drive.

Ineffective operation of the Criminal Law and inadequacy of the legal framework, rules and regulations against political corruption are main reasons why politicians continue to commit blatant anti-social acts. Stable laws, rules and regulations are needed to ensure consistent behavior and a sense of fair play, but in the Indian politics, they keep on changing as the dirty game of politics goes on.

It is a common malpractice for politicians to skimp the budget towards infrastructure spending so as to increase the opportunities for corruption.

Socio-economic factors like unemployment, illiteracy and poverty create a favorable environment for politicians to exploit the society even more. They exploit the underprivileged and uneducated by buying the media; they use the media to distort the truth about their administration and to make false promises in order to win votes from the unemployed, illiterate and poor. This distortion of information by the media also affects the educated, vigilant voters as they too don't get the truth and high-quality information that is needed to make informed choices while electing candidates.

The Right to Information Act (2005) is not suitably exercised. Moreover, the Indian citizens are not aware of its working and dynamics due to which they are not able to wield this powerful tool in exposing corruption. All laws and acts have loopholes and the RTI Act is no exception as politicians, bureaucrats and judicial officials can modify the act to escape from it. The serious attacks on information activists and deaths of information activists highlight the length to which bureaucrats, lawmakers and politicians can go to silence any opposition. This background discourages citizens to join the sincere activists and encourages the vested interests groups to carry on with their corrupt activities in an unchecked manner.

Corruption breeds corruption—corruption leads to a drastic reduction of revenues, which in turn, results in government indulging in adopting other means of raising revenues; this is a vicious cycle.

2.3 Causes of Bureaucratic Corruption—Public Office for Private Gain

Why do officials misuse public office for private gain? The modern-day Indian bureaucracy owes its origin to the colonial times when the British regime made rules as per their convenience to keep a tab over the Indians. Sadly speaking, the same scenario exists even today—the only difference is that now Indian officials are using the bureaucratic setup for exploiting their own fellow Indians—millions are at the receiving end of this phenomenon in their everyday lives.

A Word of Caution

One cause that is common to all types of corruption is the lack of awareness within the public regarding the nature of the different types of corruption. As a result of which cases of corruption, including bureaucratic corruption, go unreported.

India's bureaucracy takes its cues from the Indian politicians, who are perceived to be the most corrupt. The Indian bureaucrats follow in the footsteps of their politicians and leaders. There are ample opportunities for bureaucrats to become corrupt and one of them is imitating the acts of corrupt political leadership. The patronage of corrupt politicians and businessmen has created such a robust protection sheath around bureaucrats and public officials that even the law of the land can't touch them; hence they can get away with their acts of omission or commission.

In current times of liberalization, where businessmen can make money through unethical means, the bureaucrats too, feel that they can earn their part of the share as they are the ones who actually benefit businessmen by moving the files, fudging documents and bypassing regulations. Another cause for this deep corruption is that bureaucrats are directly involved in business ventures that they support and protect. Businesses, in turn, return the favors by letting bureaucrats join as full-time executives or as board members, which lets these bureaucrats intervene in the market directly. This intervention gives bureaucrats the distinct advantage to earn extra money from those affected by market regulations and laws. This give-and-take policy also helps businesses to save their skin from investigating agencies in the case of frauds and thefts of financial assets as the blanket of corrupt bureaucracy protects them. This exchange of corruption is cyclic in nature.

Another major cause for bureaucratic corruption is that bureaucratic agencies and officials are given monopolistic control over particular resources. The ability to intervene in markets provides them with the incentive and opportunity to extract bribes. They use this discretion and monopoly to make "convenient" interpretations of rules and regulations.

Between 1996 and 2000, the Central Vigilance Commission and the Central Bureau of Investigation investigated 13,265 individuals for corruption. Between 1998 and 2001, the Central Bureau of Investigation registered 2,256 cases under the Prevention of Corruption Act. Of these cases, 41 were from administrative departments, four were from the police and 23 from the revenue department.

Unnecessary provisions, redundant rules and complex regulations within the bureaucracy, restrict business and create huge opportunities for rent-seeking activities. Rent-seeking activities refer to soliciting and extracting 'bribe' or 'rent' for applying their legal but discretionary authority for awarding legitimate or illegitimate benefits to clients. Government setups and bureaus form special interest groups with a sole purpose of building a strong rent-seeking apparatus.

A significant portion of the national resources is placed under the direct influence of bureaucracy and also granting of business permits, quotas, government-sponsored or subsidized facilities, and licenses falls under their (bureaucrats) portfolio due to which civil officers twist and turn this aspect to their advantage by influencing the distributional outcomes in return for personal gains from the corporate community.

2.4 Causes of Corporate Corruption—A New Facet

Throughout most of the Indian corruption history, political power has dominated the scene. However, with the growth of a free market economy, a new dynamic has emerged—corporate corruption. But the seeds of corporate corruption or white-collar crime rest in the archaic tax regimes that Nehruvian socialism encouraged. In the Licence Raj days, wealth was associated with political power, but in the post-independence period, especially in the last two decades, wealth is also linked to a new dynamic—the corporate world. Free market economies, secret subsidiaries and partnerships, tax evasions, cartels, and rigid excise structures help corporate houses to pocket large price increase margins.

Corporate governance in India exists on paper only—this is both a cause and a result for the reluctance on the part of the corporate world to change for the better, which in turn, encourages them to circumvent legislation and bypass democratic processes.

The high level of corporate corruption affects the attitude of Multinational Enterprises (MNEs). On the one hand, corporate houses provide economies of scale and opportunities of growth, and on the other hand, they serve as the medium of destroying the lives of common people.

Complicate corporate ownership structures and misuse of corporate vehicles like a web of firms and trusts for avoiding the payment of taxes are a major source of corruption in corporate India. A World Bank Report of 2011 titled "The Puppet Masters: How the Corrupt Use Legal Structures to Hide Stolen Assets and What to Do About It" investigated 150 big corruption cases (cases of grand corruption) and nearly all involved use of companies in which the real ownership was concealed and this grand corruption was found to the tune of US$ 50 billion.

Corruption, especially corporate sector corruption, negatively impacts the performance of the capital market and foreign direct investment. According to the research figures, a one-point increase in the corruption can lead to a reduction in per capita foreign direct investment inflows by up to 11 percent.

Some industries are more prone to corruption due to a higher level of political and bureaucratic involvement. For example, telecom, construction, infrastructure and real estate sectors are more corrupt as there are more complex processes involved in running these businesses—to cover up phony accounting, fudged records, securities fraud, etc., to acquire several administrative approvals, to bypass regulatory compliance requirements, etc.

The political-corporate nexus leads to corruption in both the domains. Corporate funds grease the wheels of politics in order to ensure that the corporate houses can carry on with their exploits and irregularities in an unchecked manner. This nexus leads to more corporate power, and as corporate power grows, corporate corruption often follows in its path.

Corporate lobbyists and liaison agents are another agent of corruption as their sole purpose is to influence decisions and policies in favor of their corporate clients. Corporate lobbyists are paid to advocate the interests of the company they work for.

Corporate criminals are the worst and need to be punished vigorously. Despite being educated and privileged to have access to opportunities for progress, they continue to add to bad corporate governance levels.

It is important to note that causes like rigid tax structures and salary policies have become a lot more flexible in current times, yet Corporate India continues to play this unfair game. Almost a fifth of executives surveyed by Ernst & Young (Ernst & Young is a multinational professional services firm) claimed to have lost business to a competitor who paid bribes. More than a third felt corruption was getting worse.

With a more open economy, many new players enter the corporate field. As the number of players increases, the competition for limited resources becomes all the more cut-throat. And many of the players to increase their market share and sustain the competition indulge in unfair practices. For example, due to economic crunch and shortage of resources, companies bribe authorities to overlook schedule and cost overruns and sanction the next stage of controls and compliance requirements without any actions.

The monetary climate and financial structure also provide various opportunities for corporate corruption. India has a relatively high risk rating and less transparency, and these facts are testified by the presence of an inadequate setup for the protection of investors and banks, and the inefficient monitoring of business transactions. All these facts are also echoed in the Global Competitiveness Report 2007-08—it ranks corruption in India as the fourth biggest problem when doing business within India.

According to a comprehensive survey of Bribery and Corruption (2011) conducted by KPMG (KPMG is one of the leading providers of risk, financial and business advisory, internal audit, corporate governance, and tax and regulatory services) from a corporate perception standpoint, more than two-thirds of the respondents believe that India can achieve more than the projected GDP growth only if corruption is curbed.

Food for Thought

Why do corrupt and criminal enterprises need to use corruption to get their work done?

They indulge in corrupt practices both with the government and bureaucracy in order to carry out and cover up their black and grey market activities like smuggling of goods. Another example could be that of a corrupt company paying money to a public official to be included in the list of qualified bidders—in other words, the most efficient bidder is the one who would be willing to offer the highest bribe.

2.5 Questions for Reflection

A. In what ways may politicians be tempted to abuse their positions?

B. In what areas would you expect to find the worst misuse of power and position in the government?

C. Why enforcement of anti-corruption legislations has not been that effective in India?

D. Where do you see challenges in trying corruption cases?

E. Which countries are the most corrupt countries?

F. Does your company have provisions to deal with corruption?

3

Politics in India—The Abuse of Authority

We have already dealt with the main causes of political corruption in the previous chapter. Here we will delve further into the dynamics of political corruption.

According to the Transparency International Global Corruption Barometer 2010, globally, political parties are judged most affected by corruption—almost 80 percent of all respondents think they are either corrupt or extremely corrupt. Political corruption is the abuse of powers and public office by government officials for private interest and gain. India is like a snake with its tail caught in the dirty game of politics and its head entangled in the web of corruption. The widespread proliferation of corruption is majorly the end-result of politics. So much so that we are sometimes surprised when we find instances where there is no corruption occurring!

In this chapter, we will discuss the various triggers of political corruption like kleptocracy, parallel economy, competitive bribes, vote-bank politics, electoral frauds, lobbying practices, etc. Size of the government, political competitiveness, party politics, measure of personalized power wielded by politicians and many more factors determine the scale of political corruption. All these factors are discussed in this chapter.

3.1 Political Corruption—The Fuel of Corruption

Political corruption takes place at the formulation stage of politics. It refers to the misuse of political power and position. It refers to distorting or bypassing laws for private benefit or party benefit, or for the preservation and extension of power.

Both politicians and the people who elect them are not ready to learn from the pages of history. We all know why dynastic regimes and movements of the past like the French Revolution or the Roman Empire have failed...corruption. According to a survey released by a leading risk consulting firm, Kroll, in partnership with the Economist Intelligence Unit, in its annual global fraud report (2011), the corruption level in India is still amongst the highest in the world, behind Africa but in line with China, despite a slight dip in the rate of fraud. According to the 2007 Global Corruption Barometer, Indian citizens perceive the political parties as amongst the most corrupt in the country.

Political corruption not only leads to an unstable government, but also hampers economic growth and human development. In July 2008, the *Washington Post* reported that nearly a fourth of the 540 Indian Parliament members faced criminal charges—corruption being a major criminal charge. Close to half the bribes are requested by the government officials both at the state and national levels.

Herbert Werlin (1973: 73) defines political corruption as "the diversion of public resources to non-public purposes." The government funds which in reality are meant for public welfare are used to increase personal wealth. As politicians have uninhibited access to money set aside for public welfare, it becomes an easy way for them to earn extra money. This is possible as their work and the system evaluating their work are not that transparent and robust.

The socialist policies that the Indian political setup follows attract only power mongers and money-hungry citizens towards it. Candidates with real moral values and sincerity are not at all encouraged. Candidates who are willing to liaise with the mafia and have flair to play with public money are given the highest preference.

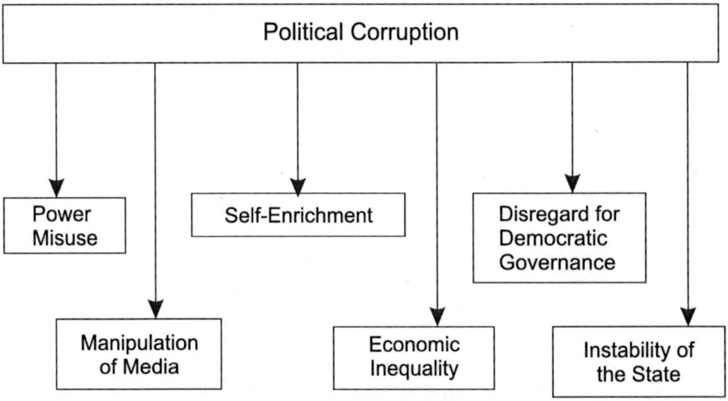

Figure 3.1: Political Corruption

3.2 Money Power in Politics—Attracts the Wrong People

The multiple political parties of the Indian political setup are constantly involved in costly electoral contests and campaigns, and to win these contests they are ready to go to any length. All Indians live and experience a corrupt democracy day in and day out. It is not only the politics played on the ground of democracy that adds to the corruption level, but also the low level of vigilance of the general masses adds to this level. The common man is not aware of the choices that he has; hence he is not able to elect morally and intellectually sincere candidates.

The nexus between corporate houses, organizations like youth forums and clubs, mafia, civil servants and the politicians is a hub of corrupt activities. Politicians have to continue patronizing these factions either in cash or in kind so that they can garner manpower and monetary reserves for future election campaigns. It is one big vicious never-ending cycle, and the common man is crushed under its wheels time and again. Instead of carrying out their duties as per their oaths and portfolios, their main job is that of returning favors and strengthening their position in party politics.

Corruption-driven ministries and ministers know that they can control the working of the anti-corruption agencies as they fall under their purview. This in itself is an incentive for politicians to practice corruption as they have no fear of accountability and transparency. These loopholes encourage politicians to play this game at a global level too. For example, several corrupt politicians generate huge amount of money from major international deals such as the purchase of arms.

Right from educational institutions and judicial officials to police force and public safety officials, the common man perceives them all as corrupt and morally aberrant entities. The reason is simple, they all mimic the corruption done by the higher-ups—the Indian politicians. If the leaders of the country are themselves going to set an incorrect example, naturally the rest are going to follow in the footsteps of their politicians and leaders. This is the charade that politics plays.

A Word of Caution

Organized loot is taking place in all the states and the government is not willing to give permission for holding a CBI probe into corruption scams running into crores of rupees—as the government itself is a major player in this loot.

3.2.1 *Flexing the Money Power Muscle—Bribes, Nepotism and More*

There are several ways of strengthening the money power muscle:

A. Bribery: It is the act of offering or receiving of a bribe. It involves payment (in cash or in kind, or returning a favor) that is taken or given in order to influence an action or decision. In the case of political corruption, in order to win a majority in elections, to get more campaign contributions, etc., politicians use tactics like kickbacks, privileges, emoluments, payoffs, etc.

B. Fraud, especially electoral fraud is termed as the worst form of corruption by some experts. Politicians indulge in all kinds of frauds involving some kind of deceit, racketeering, and counterfeiting. In electoral fraud, there is deliberate manipulation of the process of election to influence the results. Methods like fraudulent ballots, improper vote counting, rigging electronic voting machines, etc., are used to get favorable elections outcomes.

C. Embezzlement: It is theft of public resources by public officials. It is a kind of financial fraud where violation of trust and law occurs. It is when a public official misuses, converts, appropriates, steals, exchanges or disburses money or resources from the public institution in which he/she is employed for any purpose not prescribed by law.

D. Extortion: It is the practice of obtaining money, property and other resources by the use of coercion, force, violence or threat. It is also referred to as shakedown and exaction, or in common terms "pay up or else face the consequences." It is a criminal offense and yet the politicians do it on a grand scale. It is also practiced by organized crime syndicates.

E. Nepotism: This is a special form of patronage or favoritism in which a politician/official prefers his/her family members, friends and relatives regardless of merit and qualifications. For example, nominating family members to key positions in the government setup, family members are exempted from following regulations, etc. These close-knit family groups are a kind of a mafia setup, which is very difficult to break down.

F. Lobbying: It is the practice of influencing decisions made by officials in the government like influencing the choice of cabinet ministers or the economic policies. Lobbying is carried out by many types of people like government officials, legislators, private organizations, corporations and special interest groups. Recent scams like the 2G Spectrum Scam highlight the enormous clout created by the nexus of politicians, policymakers and lobbyists. This powerful clout has a wide reach and influence in almost all areas, right from retail to aviation and from infrastructure to defence. Lobbying has come a long way from individual influence-peddlers to a well-oiled parallel government and economy of liaison agents.

G. Kleptocracy: The elected officials (mis)use their position to extract resources from the governed people and to increase their political influence and personal wealth at the expense of the population. Kleptocracy leads to an authoritarian ruling class and as there is no accountability the members of the ruling class continue with their unabashed ways.

The above ways not only strengthen the money power, but also help politicians to secure their political power and position.

Political corruption lays out a wide web of deception and manipulation in the form of accumulation or extraction. Accumulation or extraction occurs when politicians abuse their powers to extract from national exchequer, private sector and from the economy at large through various techniques like embezzlement, fraud, rent-seeking, bribes, etc. Politicians also misuse their office and public money for gaining political loyalty, and for power preservation and power extension purposes, by usually deploying tactics of favoritism and patronage politics.

3.3 Impact—A Mockery of Democratic Governance

Since the 1960s, there has been constant research and study—all attempting to explain the impact and implications of political corruption. And major studies and corruption indices by the Transparency International (TI is a Berlin-based non-governmental organization that monitors corporate and political corruption), World Bank and other organizations have played an important role in providing empirical evidence of the effects and impact of political corruption across the world. According to the Transparency International Global Corruption Barometer 2010 report, under the category of institutions perceived by the respondents to be most affected by corruption, Indians perceived political parties to be the most corrupt, ranking them 4.2 on a scale of one to five.

The A.D. Gorwala Report of 1951 was one of the earliest official reports that laid bare the problem of corruption, especially corrupt political leadership that affected Indian society post-

1947. In yet another report, the Shah Commission of 1977, the corrupt political leadership in the emergency period of 1975-77 was discussed.

India has more people living in poverty than any other nation, and ironically speaking finding a solution to these basic issues of human rights has taken a backseat as the elected representatives are more interested in issues like globalization, nuclear weapons, etc. Corrupt politicians and their dirty tactics divert funds from positive investment and other productive ventures.

As of May 2011, approximately 30 percent of the total numbers of members of the Lok Sabha have criminal cases pending against them. Ironically speaking, the election rules (at the time) state that politicians may stand in elections or serve in elected positions while on trial or while appealing convictions.

Most politicians in India are involved in some form of underground banking. Underground banking is the world of hawala where money shows up in bank accounts without any paper trail—there are no bank statements or no transaction details. The money shows up within a matter of hours without any trace. Therefore, corrupt individuals are bound to join politics as they know they can adopt this route as there is no accountability involved.

Political corruption has a direct impact on education and literacy levels. Public funds are not going where they are supposed to go; they are diverted into the private coffers of political leaders. Therefore, there is a high illiteracy rate. Schools, colleges and universities are underequipped, understaffed and underfunded. The affluent manage to send their children abroad whereas the poor have to face a lot of harsh realities like their children remaining illiterate, unemployed and deprived of opportunities of growth.

People get demoralized. Citizens of the states with political corruption loose trust in their elected candidates as they are thieves of public trust of the people. Surveys reveal that political corruption has a huge corrosive effect on the civil society and its functioning. It erodes the base of good governance and the institutional values on which the economical and social growth depend. Political corruption disregards democratic values by making a mockery of democratic governance; hence there is a complete loss of faith on the part of the citizens in the entire system.

The diversion of funds also implies inadequate healthcare facilities, vaccines and drugs. This in turn leads to a number of innocent deaths due to shortage of medical aid and facilities, which in fact rightfully belongs to the citizens.

Political corruption raises the cost of doing business. Politicians are likely to introduce certain conditions to ensure that they get bribes through delays and unnecessary requirements.

Politicians use the technique of media manipulation to divert public attention from their frauds and scams to other issues and crisis. In order to serve their private interests, the politicians control the information (related to them and their offices) that the media propagates to the public through state censorship. Media manipulation destroys information credibility, which affects the voters' choice to elect able candidates and also to use the media to hold dishonest politicians accountable.

Research indicates that illegal payoffs can increase the cost and lower the quality of public works projects by as much as 30 percent to 50 percent.

Politicians and political parties have successfully helped criminalize politics and politicize crime. Political corruption in India undoubtedly exemplifies the famous adage by Lord Acton, "Power tends to corrupt and absolute power corrupts absolutely."

The complete neglect of various national issues like latest technologies, economic progress, healthcare of the citizens, environment protection, public education facilities, etc., by Indian politicians ultimately threatens the stability and survival of the state.

Food for Thought

Will progress slow corruption or will corruption slow progress?

The answer is yes to both. If we don't curb corruption, we won't be able to progress. If we don't progress, we won't be able to curb corruption.

3.3.1 *Honest Candidates are Discouraged—The Biggest Loss*

In order to do away with this rotten system, we need competent, chaste and ethical citizens. But due to corrupt politics, honest candidates never come to the fore. They fear that by entering politics they could be harmed physically for their honest ways or their reputation could be deliberately tainted in order to get rid of them. Moreover, another factor that discourages educated, honest people from entering politics is the complacent and passive citizens as they know that even if they enter politics and in times of crisis, they would not get any support from fellow citizens. Their fellow citizens are also living under constant fear and uncertainty caused by political corruption.

Illustration 3.1: Political Corruption Discourages Honest Candidates

The honest and competent citizens have a family to support; hence they need a reasonable and legitimate level of income, which is not possible in politics due to low salaries. Generally, politics attracts people who have a corrupt disposition and are willing to embezzle the national exchequer, and that is why honest, vigilant citizens are not interested in the dirty game of black money.

A Word of Caution

The Indian society has become so politicized by party affiliations that it has become virtually impossible to discuss the real issues or elect the right candidates.

3.4 Questions for Reflection

A. What do you personally believe to be the moral values that a responsible politician should be seeking to uphold?

B. How will the political corruption scenario in India change in the next 3-5 years?

C. What are the common characteristics of countries with a high degree of political corruption?

D. Do informed voters make better choices regarding their politicians?

E. Does political corruption have an effect on the daily lives of the people?

F. What is the role of culture in political corruption?

PART 2

More Faces of Corruption in India—Where We Are Now

4

Bureaucratic Corruption and More–An Arena of Hungry Hounds

We have transitioned from the Industrial Age to the era of Knowledge Workers, but still each and every aspect is being eaten away by the debilitating disease of corruption, right from food aid to admissions in schools and colleges. This chapter primarily addresses the impact of various facets of corruption in India—bribery, red-tapism, fraud and collusion of various services, bodies and institutions, both at the regional and at the national level.

What began as a way of serving the public now has become an ever-growing cancer gnawing at the very roots of morality and sincerity. Now, even deserving cases of public interest have to undergo the grind of endemic corruption; hence transforming a public office setup meant for protecting the public into an arena of hungry hounds. This scenario is prevalent in all sectors and enterprises—no exceptions there.

The chapter discusses topics like the scope of bureaucratic corruption, vulnerable sectors and institutions and many more factors. We will also discuss corruption in other fields like military, sports, etc.

Table 4.1: Corruption Perception Index and Rank of India, 1995-2002

Year	No. of Countries	Corruption Perception Index	Rank
1995	41	2.78	35
1996	54	2.63	46
1997	52	2.75	45
1998	85	2.9	66
1999	99	2.9	72
2000	90	2.8	69
2001	91	2.7	71
2002	102	2.7	71

Source: Corruption Perception Index, Transparency International, Berlin

In Table 4.1, a low CPI score on a scale of 10 means a high level of corruption. It is evident from the consistently low CPI scores of India that corruption is perceived to be rampant.

4.1 Indian Bureaucracy—Slow and Painful

According to the 2009 survey of leading economies of Asia, Indian bureaucracy is considered to be not just the least efficient in comparison to Hong Kong, Singapore, South Korea, Thailand, China, Malaysia, Indonesia, Vietnam, Philippines, Japan and Taiwan, but it was also found that working with India's civil servants was a "slow and painful" process. The 2012 survey by Political and Economic Risk Consultancy (PERC is a Hong Kong-based corporate consultancy) ranked India's bureaucracy as the worst in Asia with a score of 9.21 on a scale of 10.

Rapid economic development is a big factor for increasing the level of bureaucratic corruption. The Santhanam Committee as far back as in 1964 confirmed: "The sudden extension of the economic activities of the government with a large armory of regulations, controls, licenses and permits provided new and large opportunities" for bureaucratic corruption.

The main aim of bureaucratic corruption is to indulge in all kinds of corrupt practices to fuel the vast political machinery. Bureaucratic corruption pervades the Indian administrative system in the form of nepotism, bribery, kickbacks, irregularities, favoritism, red-tapism, etc.

Illustration 4.1: The Indian Bureaucracy—Slow and Painful

4.1.1 *Consequences, Scope and Other Factors—Detrimental All the Way*

Earlier capital controls were considered the main obstacle in the path of economic development, but now the presence of widespread bureaucratic corruption in the Indian administrative system coupled with capital controls is a huge hindrance in economic progress and also affects public policy negatively.

Just like political corruption, bureaucratic corruption affects both the quality and the quantity of public investment. For sincere corporate players, bureaucratic delays and corruption may drive them out of business, which in turn affects the consumers as they do not get access to quality products and services. Bureaucratic corruption grants monopoly position to enterprises and individuals who have the highest capacity to corrupt; hence it stifles innovation and fair competition, inhibits the growth of efficient and equitable markets, and discourages foreign direct investment.

Empirical studies have shown that bureaucratic corruption misdirects government expenditure towards less productive activities, gives rise to all kinds of unethical and illegal business practices, and creates financial repercussions for sincere investors, and this in turn, proves to be detrimental for the overall growth.

As the civil servants are responsible for the politicized resource allocation markets, entrepreneurs have to rely on them for achieving monopoly in the market. The same case applies to exempted taxes and diminished tax rates.

The actual cost of bureaucratic corruption is larger than the rent-seeking gains (bribes and transfer payments) due to the social costs involved—socially undesirable consequences. For example, when bribes are paid to public officials by unworthy contractors to win public infrastructure projects like dams, roads, etc., they have invariably led to not only property damage like collapsed bridges, but also caused a heavy loss of life. Such unfair distribution of resources could be used for investment in human capital or beneficial public programs. Another aspect of social costs is that the illegal commissions and kickbacks paid to bureaucrats add to the final cost of the government expenditures, and to match this excess expenditures someone has to pay extra revenues and that someone is the common man—the honest tax payer.

Spotlight

The level of corruption is a function of the integrity and honesty of both public officials and private individuals.

There is ample scope for bureaucratic corruption in areas of resource management and allocation, social programs, government contracts, raw materials, government funds and permits, etc. It affects individuals, firms and institutions. Forestry and logging, mining, fishing, water and gas supply, banking and insurance—you name a sector or an industry and you will find corruption ruling it.

4.2 More Corruption in India—Judiciary, Sports and More

Corruption denies the underprivileged their basic human rights and privileges, corruption breeds social and economic inequality, corruption debases the democratic practices, and corruption molds the judicial and legislative laws for the benefits of the ones in power. Right from political patronage and the lack of punitive measures to the judicial failures caused by the nexus between lawmakers and lawbreakers are dealt with to highlight the out-of-order situation. Illegal services, contracts and projects at the cost of the national exchequer and interests of the common man have become the order of the day.

A Word of Caution

All forms of corruption have their roots in the people it serves.

The India Corruption Study (2008) examined the extent of corruption in 11 government services in all the states of India. The results derived were shocking—the study found that the people living below the poverty line paid ₹ 9000 million as bribe to avail basic services like healthcare and education; services which they should have got for free.

Table 4.2: Corruption Statistics in India

Bureaucratic Corruption	795 cases were registered under the Prevention of Corruption Act in 2009 as against 744 in 2008 and 688 in 2007.
	91 percent of reported bribe demands originate from government officials.
Judicial Corruption	As per the Global Corruption Report 2007, 77 percent of persons believe the Indian judiciary is corrupt. The current state is even worst.
	As of end-2010, there were 9,927 CBI cases pending in courts.
Armed Forces Corruption	Several land scams have surfaced in the recent years. The unscrupulous armed forces officers and the land mafia collude to utilize surplus land to make a quick buck at the cost of war heroes and their grieving families.
	Corruption has not only led to delay in defense projects, but has also derailed many defense programs.
Sports Corruption	There is favoritism in all aspects, right from the selection process to awards. The national awards are not awarded to deserving and exceptional sportsmen. They are used as an instrument of favoritism by politicians.

	The epicenter of cricket betting is India; hundreds of millions of dollars are involved in the betting process, particularly when India is playing.
More Statistics	Corruption cases against government officers have risen from 17.68% in 2008 to 28.39% in 2011.
	As India boasts of 55 billionaires, about 450+ million of its people still don't have access to basic amenities.
	Real estate and related business services involving registration of property and stamp duties account for ₹ 12,534 crores.
	The total quantum of corruption money in 1990 stood at $6.3 billion and now it is more than $92 billion.

4.2.1 *Judicial Corruption—Playing with People's Lives*

The judiciary is one of the main pillars of the Indian democracy, but in the recent years a string of eye-popping scams, lengthy adjournments, fraudulent cases and fudged judgments has shattered the faith of the citizens. Instead of protecting the rights and liberties of the people from encroachments by the legislature and executive wings, the judiciary in the name of investigation allows law to take its own course, a course which is plotted by the corrupt elements.

Everything carries a price tag. The ordinary man simply cannot think of knocking the doors of justice because the system is expensive and extra time and money are needed at every step of the way, even for the non-judicial activities like registration, filing of affidavits, etc. Even sincere judicial officials fighting to serve and protect the innocent fear for their lives; they are either transferred or denied promotion or silenced for good. Even after more than 65 years of independence, there is no sign of the speedy, inexpensive justice system that the founding leaders of the nation had envisioned.

Sentences are reduced, cases are speeded up or slowed down, court funds are embezzled and evidence is omitted or admitted as per the convenience of the nexus between the judicial officials and the stronger parties. All these dirty tactics are definitely living up to the adage 'Justice delayed is justice denied.'

For filing a First Information Report or carrying out an investigation probe against Supreme Court and High Court judges, the permission of the Chief Justice of India is needed. Past experience shows that Chief Justices have hesitated in granting such permissions, which has encouraged more and more corruption in the top tier of the judiciary. Such complacency discourages the common man to raise a suspicion against a corrupt judicial official for fear that he himself may have to face contempt of court proceedings. Without systemic checks and a workable impeachment process, such cases of corruption are going to disappear into mere oblivion.

Other factors like the lack of a legal database, absence of alternative dispute resolution mechanisms, etc., have increased the capacity to seek extra income through bribes and illegal payoffs.

All these ill-practices and the misuse of discretionary powers of dispensing punishment and granting bail have been instrumental in institutionalizing corruption and its players—the charade of catching and releasing wrongdoers goes on and on.

4.2.2 *Sports—No Longer a Fair Game*

There is an even bigger player than match-fixing and doping that is hampering the Indian sports—corruption.

Players are offered large sums of money. Talent is taken over by money laundering, auctions, bookies, betting, glamour and lavish parties. Illegal betting has tarnished the sports landscape. This trend has caused so many match-fixing scams, which in turn make high profile games (matches like the Indian Premier League (IPL)) a breeding ground for corruption. Major contracts for construction of stadiums and other sports facilities are rigged by governments and companies. Players take money to fix spots and matches.

Sports being a multi-billion dollar business, instead of great performance, sports scams are hitting headlines day in and day out. With millions being gambled, money has superseded true talent.

There is an absence of accountability, transparency and strict regulations in all aspects, right from sports administration to player selection; hence no fair play.

4.2.3 *Armed Forces—The Enemy Within*

The common man looks at the Armed Forces as the last straw of hope in a corrupt system, but then even in the land of heroes there are officials who are more interested in lifestyle and luxury than in sincere duty, courage, sacrifice, bravery medals and brass-buttoned uniforms.

Corruption involving senior officers from the Indian Army, Indian Air Force and Indian Navy has shaken the public faith. Even juniors at the rank and file level are following their seniors by misusing resources. In a recent scam related to the army, a top army official alleged that he was offered a bribe by a lobbyist for approving the supply of 600 sub-standard vehicles to the army. There are gaps in the procurement and acquisition process, which have left the armed forces with old weapons and minimal safety for the country. Many officers have been caught for allegedly selling weapons in the black market. Corruption has not only led to delay in defense projects, but has also derailed many defense programs thereby compromising the nation's security. It seems the ghost of the Bofors scam still haunts the Indian Army as it sank all its plans of modernization.

Several land scams have surfaced in the recent years. Certain unscrupulous armed forces officers and the land mafia collude to utilize surplus land to make a quick buck at the cost of war heroes and their grieving families. For example, in the Adarsh Housing scandal, two former Army chiefs and one former Navy chief among others were involved.

Inquiries and probes are ordered only for show. The image of the Indian Armed Forces is tainted to such an extent that it discourages sincere and courageous candidates from joining the four wings (the Indian Army, Indian Navy, Indian Air Force and Indian Coast Guard). Even existing honest officers have lost faith in their own system.

4.2.4 *Fear-based Legalized Criminal Networks—All Over the Indian Landscape*

There is corruption all over the Indian landscape. Even the medical industry is not spared; needy people are harassed for medicines and timely treatment. Grieving families are often asked to pay bribes to obtain the death certificates of their near and dear ones. It has also crept into religious institutions; criminal and civil frauds are carried out in the name of religion. People pray to God in the morning and then indulge in corruption throughout the day. Both the religious institutions and the followers of various religions collude with the politicians to use religious differences and sentiments for vote-bank politics. Land and property scams have become the order of the day—right from registration of properties to stamp duty. Corruption in the realty sector runs deep. The collusion of financial institutions, banks, lenders and builders has shattered the home dream of the common man. The world of media is also making its presence felt on the corruption highway by accepting illegal payments in return for fudged news reports and false propaganda. Media sells its news space and channel slots for giving favorable coverage to particular individuals, corporate entities and representatives of political parties thereby refuting democratic norms. News is meant to be independent, objective, consistent and fair, but this is not the case anymore.

They all undermine the moral fiber, human rights, social justice, equal opportunities and good governance. They all are fear-based legalized criminal networks which citizens fear to approach or fight against. They all lead to a capital-starved nation. They are all a product of institutional inertia. They all undermine the efforts to reduce poverty and to promote sustainable growth.

Food for Thought

In what way are the various types of corruption related to:

Country Image
Economic Development
State Censorship of Press
Democracy
Culture
Gender

4.3 A Pictographic Recap—Corruption Dynamics at a Glance

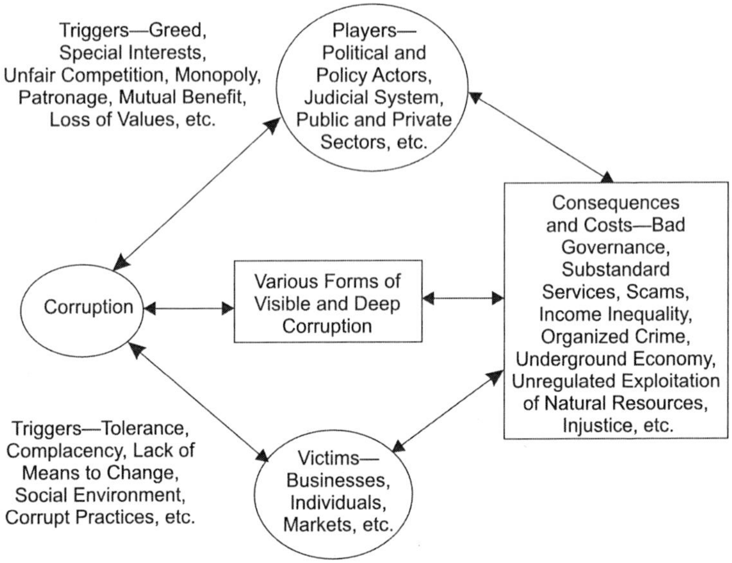

Figure 4.1: Corruption Dynamics at a Glance

4.4 Questions for Reflection

A. How serious does a corrupt act need to be before you believe it should be reported?

B. What do the corruption statistics tell us?

C. Can higher remuneration for bureaucrats reduce corruption?

D. Is corruption the main reason for the poor performance of India in sports?

E. How big a problem is judicial corruption in India?

F. At what position would you rate the corruption level in the Indian Armed Forces in comparison to other types of corruption?

G. Is bureaucratic corruption more rampant than political corruption in India?

5

The Supply Side in India—An Equal and Established Participant

Today's cut-throat competition and moral aberrations are some of the main causes of corruption as people with money and influence are given priority over people with qualifications and merit.

In the past, the common perception of corruption was that of taking and receiving bribes for illegal purposes, but today this happens in all cases—no institution or person is spared from the clutches of corruption. This chapter discusses the mindset of people who give bribes and the reasons as to why such a demoralizing mindset is being fueled.

Moral education and instilling values of honesty and integrity should begin within the four walls of each and every home in India. Only then we can act as vigilant citizens and prevent fair setups from degenerating into pits of corruption. This chapter deals with how cultural contamination and the degradation of the moral landscape leads to corrupt practices, but it also ends on a hopeful note by discussing how the equation of Encouraging Ethics=Combating Corruption can be realized.

Just as corruption begins at home, so does moral education. In the earlier chapters, we dealt with the demand side, in this chapter we will talk about the supply side and also how morals can help to curb both the ends.

Spotlight

Martin Luther King always dreamt of a world where men would be judged not by the color of their skin, but by the content of their character. It is up to each and every individual to build up a strong character and moral values.

5.1 The Facilitators—The Other Side of the Coin

The demand side represents people and institutions that practice corruption whereas the supply side comprises people and institutions that provide opportunities for corrupt dealings and facilitate corruption. Corruption from the supply side is generally given so-called respectable terms as consultancy fees, commission, etc. A clear understanding of the linkage between the demand and supply sides of corruption is critical for designing a more balanced anti-corruption approach.

Traditionally speaking, bribe payers in India have been viewed as victims of the system, due to which there is no supply side culpability. But in current times, the supply side is no longer a victim—rather corporate entities and individuals, both big and small, are more than willing to play this game of corruption. Earlier the private sector and corporations were perceived as a victim of corruption, but this is not the case anymore. In current times of liberalization, they too are an equal participant in the corruption process. The Maoist insurgency is one such glaring example of what corrupt practices by companies can do. Corruption in India has set a new standard with the 210+ billion dollars coal scam, and now with the scale and magnitude of this mother of all scams, the supply side of the corruption equation definitely cannot be ignored with more than 100 companies, both private and state-owned involved in this scam.

Corruption has both demand and supply sides to it. Most of the academic literature on corruption studies focuses on the demand side, but in my book we will talk about the supply side as well. The role of individuals and organizations (corporate houses, public relations professionals, media and journalists, pressure groups, non-governmental organizations, retired Indian Civil Service and Indian Administrative Service officers, think-tanks, etc.) in the supply side of corruption should not be overlooked or underestimated. It is not just the bribe takers alone but also the briber payers who are equally responsible for corruption. According to the Bribe Payers Index 2011 Report, the supply side of corruption in India has a score of 7.5 and it is ranked at position 19.

On the one hand, the demand side undermines the Indian constitution, legal system and democracy, and on the other hand, the supply side symbolizes the destruction of morality and honesty. The demand side is nullifying the principles of establishing a moral society, whereas the supply side is nullifying the society itself.

Corruption of morals deters and discourages the honest and the bright human resources from contributing their skills, ideas, etc., to enrich the society. These days, people and organizations in India are resorting to different ways and means to gain leverage due to heightened unfair competition and exposure to globalization.

The supply side along with the demand side has adverse social effects. Both the sides dissuade people from coming together for a good cause. They instill a complacent attitude and disunity among people, which results in a weak and fragmented civil society.

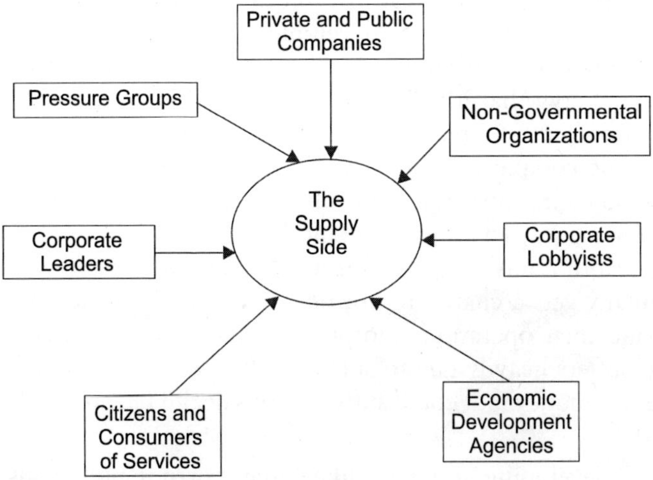

Figure 5.1: The Supply Side Players

5.2 Causes of Supply Side Corruption—A Vicious Cycle

Corruption is a two-way street. Corruption is a vicious cycle, and both the demand side and supply side are turning its wheels more vigorously now than ever. As corruption takes place at the interface of the public and private sectors, understanding the dynamics of both the sides is very important.

Those who pay bribes are sometimes depicted as innocent parties, but that is not the case always. The fact is that both sides involved are either directly or indirectly laundering resources and are causing suffering to the public. Previously, the supply side believed that corruption exists because of the demand side and did not consider itself as player in the game of corruption. Over the years, the supply side, too, has become an equal and established participant in corruption.

So far we have discussed the causes of corruption in regards to the demand side—the receivers. In this sub-section, we will deal with the supply side causes to present a balanced view of the matter. It is not always the case that the givers are the sufferers. For example, when a bureaucrat and a business executive are involved, they collude because they have a common purpose to serve. The bureaucrat wants his share of the deal, whereas the executive wants to carry out his business operations without any hassles. In the process, they both benefit at the cost of the public. In fact, in poor or developing countries, both local and multinational organizations tend to initiate the corruption process as they know that it is hard for ill-paid public officials to resist the opportunity of making extra money. For example, a foreign medicine company strikes a deal with the health minister of a developing country for launching medicines at a cheap price, even if the medicines are not suitable for the country's citizens. The health ministry gets its cut of the deal, whereas the foreign company gets a chance to not only make more profits, but also expand their operations footprint. In the process, the common man suffers heavily due to substandard medicines—he not only loses his money, but could suffer serious health hazards including death.

In developing countries like India, corrupt politicians and government officials receive bribes totaling between 20-40 billion

US dollars annually, this grand corruption actually represents a loss of more than 20 percent to 40 percent of positive progress. Supply side, too, is equally responsible for this repercussion and loss. With the rise of globalization and foreign trade, the grand corruption from the supply side players like international corporations has increased, and India is one lucrative playground for playing this grand (corruption) game.

While there has been a significant change in attitude towards corruption, many players of the supply side still continue to go with the status quo—corruption is an accepted part of life. This is so very true for the business players as they feel that it is a survival need to follow corrupt practices in order to keep up with competition. For them corruption is a very lucrative investment.

Factors like the never-ending greed for materialistic pleasures, degradation of the family system, and the theories of caste and psychology behind societal corruption are responsible for an increase in the supply side.

Vested interest groups fuel the supply side all the more as they want to capture a larger share of the market and pocket all the profits. They inhibit the proper functioning of markets.

The Indian culture is both tolerant and forgiving in nature and due to these inherent factors, deviances in personal and public life are both accepted and forgiven. The same holds true for the supply side and demand side of corruption.

Spotlight

Over the years, the private sector has been established as an equal participant in the corruption process.

High tax rates increase the tendency of not to pay taxes and not to comply with the tax laws of the country, and this is achieved by resorting to black money inflows exchanged between the givers and takers. A report submitted by the National Institute of Public Finance and Policy (NIPFP) to the finance ministry estimated that black money would exceed 10 percent or more of GDP; this study was commissioned by NIPFP in last week of December 2012 in order to quantify the black money that was generated in India.

Though there are legal and regulatory frameworks being developed and adopted around the world, including India, their implementation is not that smooth, and due to which there are challenges involved in curbing the supply side corruption. Low penalties, ineffective civil society organizations and a weak judicial system let the supply side continue with their corrupt behaviors.

Entrepreneurs and corporate houses are major players on the supply side. In order to minimize the burden of regulations and to gain access to government-sponsored subsidies, they invest heavily in underhand dealings with the government and civil servants. They avoid and evade their responsibilities to the society that actually sustains them.

The lack of honest, strong and independent audit firms and oversight institutions, the lack of strict implementation of code of ethics and the lack of media's social responsibility pave the way to making supply side corruption easier.

5.2.1 *Curbing the Supply Side—Tackling Corruption from All Sides*

Over the years, Indian anti-corruption measures have mainly focused on the demand side of corruption, but now, India also needs to focus on the supply side. Just as leaders in the public and private sectors, whistleblowers, concerned citizens and RTI activists are showing courage in curbing the demand side, similarly, they need to stand against the supply side too. The participation of the corporate entities and private sector in the fight against corruption is critical to success.

Corruption, whether supply side or demand-driven, is not merely a result of the lack of morality, but also due to institutional failures. A reliable system of incentives for transparency and honesty will help to encourage moral behaviors. There needs to be a private sector approach towards fighting the supply side—the private sector needs to actively engage itself against corruption.

Special anti-graft legislations, laws and initiatives targeted at corrupt practices related to international and national trade need to be formulated and strictly adhered to. Though the judicial and legal mandate in India has provisions to deal with the supply side like the private sector, these provisions are limited in scope and are not strictly implemented due to oversight and gaps in implementation policies.

India needs to impose tougher penalties and sentences on the supply side of corruption. The United States' Foreign Corrupt Practices Act and related laws in other OECD (Organization for European Economic Co-operation and Development) countries are the primary supply-side anti-corruption measures that India needs to study and adapt these to her problems. Hong Kong's Prevention of Corruption Ordinance, United Kingdom's Bribery Act 2010 and America's Anti-bribery Act are other good models to follow. Recent media articles have indicated that the Union Home Ministry is working on adding a chapter in the Indian Penal Code to tackle corruption in the private sector, which could potentially apply to transactions between two private entities as well. Corporate experts also echo the same opinion that it is high time that India has laws with a clear focus on the corruption in the corporate sector.

Another area that needs to be monitored closely is corporate lobbying. The Radia Tapes controversy clearly shows the gaps and gray areas in legislation; there is no legal provision that directly deals with malpractices in lobbying and public relations. Corporate lobbyists need to be brought under the scanner through a Lobbyist Act that requires all corporate lobbyists to register and report their financial activities and transactions. This is the first step in dealing with industrial houses that employ lobbyists to influence government policies for their own benefits. Canada's Lobbying Act and America's Lobbying Disclosure Act are good examples to follow.

A Word of Caution

India needs to study all the global models, legislations, acts, etc., and then use them as a template and as a starting point, and alter them to tackle local problems and issues of the supply side.

Independent Economic Journalism plays an active role in exposing supply side scams. Media professionals and journalists should be trained and equipped with the tools of analysis to investigate scams. Freedom of information should be strengthened so that a free media can perform its role as a vigilant watchdog without fear of reprisal.

Major industry bodies like the Confederation of Indian Industry and National Association of Software and Services Companies are among the top lobby groups and industry advocates. If these top associations themselves advocate fair policies and practices, the rest of the business world too will be able to adopt fair dealings. In the case of non-ethical business practices and corrupt organizations, the Securities and Exchange Board of India, the capital market regulator, should blacklist and penalize the defaulters through penalties, criminal sanctions, debarments, etc.

The level of good corporate governance needs to be pushed up by the corporate world and industry champions. Corporate houses need to introduce corporate social responsibility and self-regulation initiatives, and projects and porgrammes that involve their employees and employee representative bodies like trade unions to monitor their own businesses, carry out their business transactions according to the business standards and laws, and that too in full honesty and transparency, and also to cooperate with law enforcement agencies. A combination of internal and external factors and a coalition of public and private stakeholders are needed to achieve the highest standards of corporate governance. Corporate leadership examples that condemn corruption will set best standards of ethical corporate behaviors and also put peer pressure on rival companies to follow these standards.

The Indian Government completed the process of ratification of the United Nations Convention Against Corruption (UNCAC) in 2011, six years after signing this convention. UNCAC is the first globally legally binding international anti-corruption instrument; it is a landmark convention not only in terms of its wide coverage but also for its provisions and practices like tracing, freezing and confiscating the proceeds of corruption, sharing good practices, comprehensive set of standards, rules and measures for strengthening legal and regulatory regimes to fight corruption, research, peer reviews, training, etc.

This transnational move is an important milestone in India's role in the global economy and in combating the supply side of the corruption equation in order to minimize the loss of current and future business. This move will help India to seize unlawful money and assets and to deal with the problem of black money and corruption through administrative reforms and legislative measures. This convention requires criminalizing the act of foreign bribery; hence the Indian Government has drafted the Prevention of Bribery of Foreign Public Officials and Officials of Public International Organizations Bill 2011. This Bill empowers the Indian Government to enter into agreements with other nations for enforcing this law and for exchanging investigative information. It criminalizes the acceptance or solicitation of bribes by both foreign public officials and officials of public international organizations for obtaining or retaining business as well as abetting or attempting the above acts.

The Global Compact Anti-Corruption Principle is derived from the United Nations Convention Against Corruption. This principle encourages businesses to adopt sustainable and socially responsible policies in the areas of labor, environment, human rights and anti-corruption. India is a part of the anti-corruption collective action initiative for implementing this principle. India needs to show sustained political commitment so as to increase awareness of the anti-corruption acts and strategies among the key stakeholders in India including the government setup, business world, media, human rights groups, civil society, and international development agencies. As India is an emerging export power, it is crucial for it to strengthen its domestic supply side anti-corruption strategies and then extend them beyond the borders to curb corruption occurring at the national and international interfaces of trade and business in order to achieve openness to investment and trade from overseas. India can achieve this goal by adopting various global voluntary standards and business principles.

Table 5.1: Power Words to Fight Supply Side Corruption

Civil Activism	Corporate Governance
Societal Reforms	An Engaged Society
Strict Implementation of Code of Ethics	Public Education and Mobilization
Good Morals	Employee Participation
A Human Rights-based Approach	A Private Sector Approach
Institutional Reforms	Anti-graft Legislations
Global Models	A Strong Internal Intent
Economic Journalism	A Coalition of Public and Private Stakeholders

5.3 Good Morals—Corruption Begins at Home, so does Moral Education

A value-oriented family unit is one where one is taught to fulfill one's duty towards society and nation in all sincerity; this is where the character building process occurs. Several such value-oriented family units create a community of morally responsible citizens, and when such communities come together they lead to the creation of a broader society that is capable of imbibing thoughts, actions, beliefs and behaviors that are ethically appropriate, and also is capable of resisting corruption and acting against it.

Dealing with corruption, especially the supply side of it, needs a "culture of reforms"—both institutional reforms and societal reforms. We have already dealt with the institutional reforms in the previous section, but what will make them successful are societal reforms. Societal reforms in the form of societal changes like a proper mindset of all stakeholders, appropriate cultural and attitudinal changes, moral values, human-based approach, civil activism, a strong internal intent and a multidisciplinary approach.

An anti-corruption culture through values-based education is the need of the hour. Anti-corruption education begins at home and can be enriched and sustained by youth education clubs in business schools, colleges, universities and corporate houses, and then finally disseminated to the masses through public education and public mobilization programs.

Parents need to set good examples of ethical behaviors through their own thoughts, actions and decisions, which then their children can imbibe and apply in all the spheres of life. To support and nourish the home efforts, India needs to set up a 'Fight Corruption Through Moral Education Division,' which can adopt a multi-thronged approach by involving the citizens, educational institutions and corporations across the length and breadth of the country to build resistance against corruption, to educate the masses about their civil rights, and to instill in the citizens a sense of duty and responsibility towards their community and nation. An engaged society creates the base of good morals—good morals lead to the reduction of corruption from the supply side (and even the demand side), considerably.

Illustration 5.1: Crush the Cancer of Corruption Within

Food for Thought

How important do you think are the following values for being a morally and ethically responsible citizen? Rate them on a scale of 1 to 5—1 not at all important as it is a negative value and 5 being highly important as it is a positive value.

Respect for Law
Honesty
Tolerance
Fairness
Complacency
Sense of Justice
Favoritism

5.4 Questions for Reflection

A. To what extent does your country's constitution enable you to take a proactive role towards fighting corruption?

B. Why have there been so few successful attempts to curb corruption?

C. Do you think that the anti-corruption strategy of India does not adequately focus on minimizing the supply side of corruption?

D. Is it valid to say that in India the bribe givers continue to lead a scot-free life?

E. Should lobbying in India be formally recognized?

F. What can employees do to curb the supply side of corruption?

G. Why do some companies engage in cross-border corruption, while others do not?

H. Do schools and colleges in India provide values-based education to help the youth fight against corruption?

I. How does moral corruption affect people's lives?

PART 3

The Indian Anti-Corruption Aspirations—Where We Need To Be

6

Curb Corruption—Anti-Corruption Efforts

Fighting corruption is not something that we can leave entirely for the government machinery to handle. It is we common people who are threatened by it and when the law-makers and protectors themselves are taking us for granted, we need to step up and abolish corruption and grow mutually in the positive sense through the bonds of cooperation. Finally, curbing corruption is about empowering vulnerable groups and victims of corruption through human rights, access to up-to-date, complete, truthful and understandable (non-technical) information, participation, and social justice.

Either the common man is not aware of the various dangerous dimensions of corruption or he has simply given into its clutches without even trying to change the situation. With a committed will and a feeling of unity, we as citizens of India and of the world, can start a whole new process of reversal. This is where collective movements and mass initiatives against corruption come into the picture.

6.1 A Multi-pronged Approach

For minimizing the dangerous impact and reach of corruption, we need to combine societal and institutional efforts and initiatives—a multi-pronged approach is the need of the hour. We need to pinpoint and study those scenarios where there is a corruption-free environment and replicate the same across the society. For achieving this environment, we need strong legislations.

Apart from the aspect of how the rise of anti-corruption came about to be, this chapter discusses the measures to combat corruption and to challenge government bodies and corporate entities responsible for moral degradation. All the anti-corruption measures and strategies may not entirely stop corruption but can reduce its incidence to a considerable extent.

Since 2011, India has witnessed an intense anti-corruption campaign, more of a massive social movement. The Indian anti-corruption laws need to keep in line with such massive movements. Although many important landmarks have occurred over the years, the laws enacted while India was under British control need to shed their colonial layers and adapt themselves to the modern-day corruption dynamics. There are also several anti-corruption agencies, police and courts in India (in states like Karnataka and Andhra Pradesh) that need to constantly upgrade themselves to adapt to modern corruption scenarios and such successful initiatives need to be replicated in other Indian states too.

6.1.1 *Transparency in Administration*

Corruption in India has become a low-risk, high-profit business in India, and one of the main factors for this is the lack of transparency in administration.

There is a need to change the judicial system in so far as corruption cases are concerned, including corruption cases involving judicial officials. In recent times, the working of the judges of superior courts has come under intense scrutiny. As a reaction to these concerns, the Judicial Standards and Accountability Bill was introduced in the Lok Sabha on December 1, 2010. This bill requires judges to declare their assets, lays down judicial standards, and establishes processes for removal of judges of the Supreme Court and High Courts. However, this bill has been criticized on several accounts like the scheme for filing complaints, atmosphere of secrecy, etc. According to experts adopting such bills and structures from other nations without considering the constitutional setup and the unique conditions existing in India will only damage the credibility of the entire system.

There needs to be a transparent system of social audits in place that will relax restrictions on the release of information, facilitate increased information sharing and provide access to data on corruption convictions and prosecutions. The possibility of such an open access would in itself serve as a means to deter corruption and help to prevent corruption at all points of decision-making. The Indian Government has to a certain extent addressed this aspect through citizen charters, e-governance initiatives and the Right to Information Act.

Citizens are entitled to know the reasons, facts and the basis of the policies drafted and decisions taken by the administration. Such an approach will minimize red-tapism considerably and it needs to be adopted soon. The Indian Administration setup should encourage active transparency where administrative officials or representatives publish the data and information about the state's affairs proactively rather than solely relying on passive transparency where the information is shared or published on request. On the one hand, the Supreme Court of India recently granted constitutional status for the right to know, whereas on the other hand, the Official Secrets Act (OSA), 1923 (OSA is an anti-espionage act from the British colonialism era) poses a conflict with the Right to Information Act as clause 6 under OSA states that information from any governmental office is considered official information, hence it can be used to override the Right to Information Act 2005 requests. Such colonial legislations need to be done away with in order to tackle modern-day scenarios of corruption.

6.1.2 *Robust Legislative Framework*

A robust legislative and institutional framework is one of the key parameters for the effective implementation of the anti-corruption mandate and anti-corruption laws.

A strong framework also means that the political and legislative interference is minimal when it comes to matters related to the operations of anti-corruption agencies and bodies. Several corruption studies indicate a reverse picture wherein interference occurs at every step of the way, right from appointments to these bodies' day-to-day work—this is true for India too—for example, the Central Bureau of Investigation (CBI), a premier investigating agency in India, is subject to legislative and political manipulation. Instead of manipulation and interference, the political setup and legislative framework should provide resources for increasing the technical capacity and technical expertise to assist CBI in successful investigation.

The Indian Government should engage in high-level policy dialog with other nations, donors and relevant stakeholders of the society, review existing laws and reforms in order to refine country-led anti-corruption efforts and restructure itself in such a way that the government will able to address the various levels of corruption and the responses to these levels as they will vary from institution to institution, sector to sector and state to state. These government-initiated steps are necessary to replace self-serving ends with public-serving ends. In 2010, the Central Vigilance Commission unveiled the long-awaited long-term governmental anti-corruption initiative, the Draft National Anti-Corruption Strategy. The Draft National Anti-Corruption Strategy aims at creating a legal and regulatory anti-corruption framework and strengthening the existing institutions to effectively combat corruption. It addresses issues like political and administrative corruption, social infrastructure for fighting corruption, role of citizens in anti-corruption, and role of the private sector in combating corrupt. This draft piece of legislation is expected to increase the role of institutions such as the Central Bureau of Investigation (CBI), Comptroller and Auditor General (CAG), Central Vigilance Commission (CVC), as well as various anti-corruption agencies.

Legislative oversight over the bureaucratic setup is essential. The Indian legislative framework should also have strong financial disclosure laws to improve accountability. Such laws require government officials to declare their incomes and assets and this will in turn act as a deterrent for corruption. Again such laws need to have a provision for public access and verification.

Important pieces of anti-corruption legislation like the Judges (Inquiry) Bill, Benami Transactions (Prohibition) Bill, Lokpal Bill and Corrupt Public Servants Bill have been pending for quite some time. Such pending bills need to be legislated into acts to address various aspects of corruption in India. Citizen groups need to engage and make their views heard on such bills in order to address the various aspects of corruption. The Judges (Inquiry) Bill aims at bringing greater transparency in the judiciary and making the judges more accountable. This bill is aimed to introduce an inquiry mechanism for allegations and complaints against members of the judiciary. The Benami Transactions (Prohibition) Bill, 2011, prohibits all persons from entering into benami transactions (property transactions in the name of another person). Any benami property shall be confiscated by the Central Government. It seeks to replace the existing Benami Transactions (Prohibition) Act, 1988. The new Bill offers a wider scope; it contains elaborate provisions dealing with the definition of benami transaction and benami property, prohibited benami transactions, consequences of entering into a prohibited benami transaction and the procedure for implementing the benami law. The Lokpal Bill is supposed to address corruption in high offices, including the office of the Indian Prime Minister.

There is a lack of transparency in electoral funding. For example, there are currently no regulations that require parties or candidates to disclose funding or donations. Electoral reforms are urgently needed to eliminate the influence of unaccounted funding and donations, prevent the compromise of the integrity of policy-making and disqualify candidates with criminal records from contesting election. Such loopholes need to be immediately addressed.

Until recently, government servants on the verge of retirement could manage to escape proceedings for minor penalty. The Group of Ministers (GoM) decided that mere retirement should not be a ground for dropping proceedings against corrupt government servants. A cut in pension up to 10 percent may be imposed in case of minor penalty for a period not exceeding five years. The existing major penalty of compulsory retirement with full benefits may be changed to compulsory retirement along with a provision that the competent authority may impose up to 20 percent cut in pension. Such measures will definitely help in strengthening the vigilance administration.

6.1.3 *Civil Society, Civic Monitoring and Participatory Process*

External scrutiny and objective analysis are essential for assessing government laws and reforms—this is where the civil society comes into the picture. The last decade has seen the rise of civil society initiatives and NGOs engaged in anti-corruption work at the village, city, state and national levels across India. Although there are a large number of civil society organizations in India, the participation level of the citizens is still quite low. Moreover, on several occasions sincere civil society exponents have been beaten up, prosecuted by authorities or brutally murdered, which again discourages the common man to join such organizations and movements. But the 2011 mass civil society movement definitely indicates that the civil society is no longer willing to be taken for granted.

Tools like public debates, information leaflets, educational campaigns, citizen advisory boards, outreach programmes, national integrity workshops and documentaries can be used to include more and more citizens in the civil society's fight against corruption and stimulate demand for reform within the citizens. The Indian civil society players need to join hands with the private sector efforts and international pressure groups to expand the vision of the public domain. Civil participation is also needed for detection and prevention of unaccounted money and bringing the same into the mainstream economy.

Apart from ordinary citizens, even civil servants need to rise to the occasion. There have been several daring traditional civil servants in India who have made the cry against corruption their personal crusade. In recent years, many brave civil servants have created the wave of new policy entrepreneurs, who are not only identifying gaps in anti-corruption reforms and policies, but also giving inputs to the government for developing new policy instruments to fill these gaps.

Civic monitoring provides value-added support to the civil society's anti-corruption efforts and bolsters the growth of civil society networks. Mobile monitoring is a beneficial way of civic monitoring and reporting of corrupt activities. As Indians are mobile-savvy, they need to utilize this quality for good purposes (instead of endless messaging and chatting). Vigilant citizens can capture videos of corrupt officials indulging in corrupt practices and then they can either approach civil society organizations, or they can share these videos through various social networking sites, or they can even send it to the higher authorities. Civic monitoring should come in the form of public perceptions too and this can be achieved through integrity surveys. The findings of these surveys should be shared with leadership, which the leaders then can use to draft action plans for tackling corruption.

Civic oversight monitoring of local activities, provincial administration, public institutions, government policies and practices through citizens' initiatives and community leaders is highly needed in India. For this to work, India needs to provide comprehensive training on oversight monitoring skills, coalition-building, monitoring tools and corruption indicators to the civic leaders and civic groups so that they would be able to provide an excellent mechanism for influencing the national agenda on combating corruption.

Spotlight

New forms of political participation through the civil society are needed to increase the level of democratic engagement and citizen-state interaction.

Civic monitoring should be formally recognized as a key player in developing, implementing and sustaining an anti-corruption strategy.

The professional capacity of the civil society needs to be increased through technical assistance, feedback mechanisms and task forces to be effective champions of anti-corruption and to be able to push the goals of anti-corruption in the political agenda. Coordination of the civil society with other bilateral and multilateral NGOs, media professionals, business and professional associations, and civic advocacy organizations is necessary for fostering the attitude of anti-corruption within the Indian citizens.

Media involvement through various platforms like print, radio, television and online is a must. Vigilant ombudsmen in media and better self-regulation are necessary to curtail the nuisance of the "paid news" corrupt practice, especially during election campaigns and therefore also referred to as "electoral malpractice." However, self-regulation only offers a limited solution to the problem since there would always be wrongdoers. Politicians, media companies and the Press Council of India need to realize that in the long term such malpractices undermine not just democracy but also the credibility of the politicians and media as well. At times, the government uses its power under the Official Secrets Act to censor security-related articles. Civil society and human rights groups' oversight can also reduce the degree of this problem, but only to an extent.

Building anti-corruption advocacy and strengthening the political and institutional stability through a participatory process is the key to achieving a society-driven plan for designing and implementing anti-corruption policies. A participatory process and social consensus are needed to create a deeper, shared understanding of corruption. The depth and breadth of participation will increase only when the involved stakeholders learn to become non-tolerant towards corrupt power structures (visible, invisible and hidden power).

6.1.4 *Social Responsibility and Moral Values Propagation*

Corruption can be minimized through the propagation of social responsibility and moral values. Merely introducing codes of conduct to promote professional ethics in the government and bureaucracy is not enough. These ethics need to be practiced by everyone in everyday life too. The Indian Ministry of Education should further the cause of instilling moral values in the future workforce and future students in order to create faith-based organizations and an incorruptible society. It is about fighting corruption right from the classrooms.

The citizenry needs to be sensitized and informed about corruption. Extensive public education and awareness programs need to be designed with a focus on specific target groups at various levels. For example, at school level, students can be introduced to corruption and its dynamics and how to deal with them through documentaries, discussions and role play exercises. Such techniques will help to inculcate moral values from a very young age itself and also help younger minds to analyze and recognize sources of corruption, help them to realize the significant pay-offs of a relatively corruption-free society, and also help them to make moral distinctions between the right and the wrong aspects of life. The current Indian educational system lays emphasis on worldly education (reading, writing, etc.). The system needs to be revamped to include moral values in the education curriculum. Worldly education makes a man great, whereas moral values make a man spiritually good and socially responsible.

The Indian religious community too should place greater emphasis on promoting moral values in everyday life. The Indian corporate and political spheres need to create role models for guiding society, especially the youth. The Indian youth are attracted to politicians, corporate bigwigs and film actors; hence it is the moral duty of such high-profile public figures to set good examples of moral values and social responsibility (and not otherwise)—everybody needs to get away from the page three culture.

6.1.5 *Access to Human Rights and Justice*

According to the Preamble of the Declaration of Human and Citizens Rights, 1789, "Ignorance, forgetfulness or contempt for human rights are the only causes of public misfortune and the corruption of governments." As corruption not only affects the political and economic spheres but also corrodes human rights and fundamental freedoms, it is essential for India to adopt a human rights-based approach for handling corruption and for protecting disadvantaged people, vulnerable communities and marginalized groups. Such an approach will bring new actors and a broader spectrum of perspectives into play, which can compel the Indian setup to tackle forms of corruption that harm people who are either marginalized or under-privileged.

The integration of human rights and justice in the anti-corruption agenda will also help to control the allocation, accessibility and accountability of public resources, especially when it comes to marginalized and victimized people.

India needs to think beyond mere criminal laws—India needs to adopt a broader perspective by analyzing the role of human rights and justice. There has to be a two-way link for minimizing corruption even further—making anti-corruption tools and mechanisms easily accessible to human rights and justice advocates and also making humans rights and justice bodies easily accessible to anti-corruption and human rights advocates.

The Human Rights Front, a division of the Anti-Corruption Front (an initiative of the All India Anti-Corruption Press and the Journalists Foundation), aims to follow, adopt and promote the Universal Declaration of Human Rights of the United Nations, Indian Constitution and National-International Law. It awards "The Outstanding Contribution to the Anti-Corruption Movement" to an individual or representatives of the state institutions, NGOs, business sector, media, and national and international organizations, who have shown relentless dedication in combating corruption in India.

A Word of Caution

Anti-corruption advocates and human rights advocates should ensure that their own actions and judgments do not produce forms of "invisible" power that nullify human rights and justice.

India needs to encourage dialogue between national anti-corruption organizations and human rights agencies in understanding their common role and establishing working relations as the fight against corruption and the struggle to promote human rights and justice share a great deal of common ground. They are inextricably linked and interdependent and both the elimination of corruption and the strengthening of human rights require a strong integrity system (Laurence Cockcroft, TI Working Paper, 1998). The right to a corruption-free society should be considered a fundamental human right so that everyone enjoys an equal status in the cultural, economic, civil, social and political fields.

The concept of Citizen's Charter helps to improve the quality of public services. It ensures accountability, transparency and the quality of goods and services provided by various government organizations. The Government of India has tabled the Citizen's Charter and Grievance Redressal Bill 2011 (also known as The Right of Citizens for Time Bound Delivery of Goods and Services and Redressal of their Grievances Bill or the Citizens Charter Bill). This Bill seeks to confer on every Indian the right to get delivery of specified goods and services within the stipulated time frame and to provide a time-bound mechanism for grievance redressal. The Bill makes it mandatory for every public authority to publish a Citizen's Charter within six months of the commencement of the Act, failing which the penalty for failure to deliver would include fines and disciplinary proceedings. Effective implementation of such Citizen's Charters across the nation will go a long way in controlling corruption.

6.1.6 *Protection of Whistleblowers*

Access to information should be the rule; secrecy should be the exception. This access to information is provided by whistleblowers. Whistleblowers are those people who expose corruption with an aim and a hope that justice would be served. In the last few years, several Indian whistleblowers have made an impact in exposing the excessive discretionary authority of public officials. However, on the one hand, whistleblowers and citizens have access to records through the RTI and on the other hand, this access is not backed by sufficient level of protection and accountability.

Despite the fact that the protection of whistleblowers has improved since the Dubey case in 2003, according to an October 2011 article by Bloomberg (Bloomberg is a multinational mass media corporation based in New York City), at least 12 whistleblowers were killed since January 2010, while at least 40 people were assaulted after seeking information under the law. These figures indicate that there are still institutional flaws in the Whistleblowers Protection Act, 2011.

The Central Vigilance Commission (CVC) can now take action against anyone who leaks names of whistleblowers and witnesses and can request police assistance to investigate complaints. The CVC provides a secure whistleblower/complaint mechanism for exposing corruption and has received over 1,300 complaints since the Public Interest Disclosure and Protection to Persons Making the Disclosure's (PIDR) passing in 2005. Despite the (supposedly) confidential PIDR complaints, the CVC reports that some 30 whistleblowers have suffered from harassment or victimization. The Public Interest Disclosure and Protection to Persons Making the Disclosure Bill does provide some level of protection, but again there are flaws in it too.

Properly implemented witness protection programs and acts are needed in India. A complete lack thereof causes many witnesses to turn hostile. Proper provisions in terms of witness identity protection, streamlined procedural laws, payment of allowances to the witnesses, etc., and a witness-friendly environment should be provided right from the police stations to court premises to facilitate the witnesses to testify.

Research figures and evidence show that citizens, and particularly disadvantaged groups, are often unaware of the existence of laws on the right of access to information in India. The Right to Information Act (RTI) was enacted in 2005, but knowledge of the law remains poor. With such poor knowledge, there is bound to be lack of public debate and consultation on any bill related to information access and whistleblowers protection, and therefore there is always a fear that such a bill will become another 'paper tiger.'

The Right to Information Act 2005 has reportedly improved bureaucratic transparency by giving citizens better access to information and records. However, according to Freedom House 2009, those who try to expose corruption within the bureaucracy often receive threats or are otherwise penalized in terms of career prospects. In recent times, RTI activists have demanded a stronger whistleblower law, including provisions for accountability and compensation for victims.

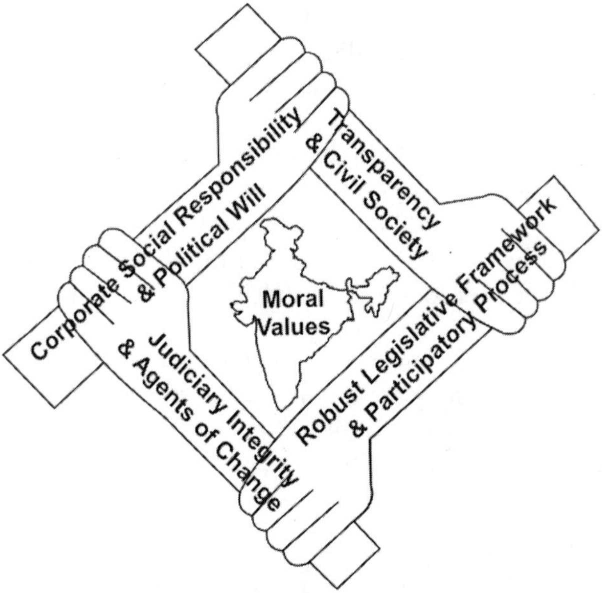

Illustration: 6.1: The Anti-Corruption Measures

Food for Thought

Rank the following anti-corruption measures from 1 to 10 to indicate the level of importance and effectiveness. 1 being the least important and effective and 10 being the most important and effective.

Protection for whistleblowers

Greater transparency

Tougher legislation

Special anti-corruption courts

Greater access to government information

Watchdog institutions like civil society

Ethical norms and codes of conduct

Government oversight over government activities

School-level propagation of moral values

Access to human rights and justice

6.2 India Against Corruption—The Crusaders

There are numerous Indian heroes standing up for the rights of the common man by trying to purge corruption from the office peon to the topmost babu. They epitomize the essence of a corruption-free society. In this chapter, it is my earnest attempt to present these heroes and their fight against corruption and honest efforts in reforming India's governance.

By sharing the information about the efforts put in by these heroes, I hope to encourage one and all to leverage their messages and contribute to the whole movement in order to create and sustain democratic governance that is not only efficient and effective, but also fully accountable to the nation. These beacons of hope echo one common thread that the responsibility to fight corruption is upon every Indian. Every Indian must say "No" to corruption.

6.2.1 *Anna Hazare—The New Face of Anti-Corruption*

The 2011 protests in India have given the modern-day anti-corruption drives a new face—Kisan Baburao Hazare, popularly known as Anna Hazare or simply Anna (Anna means "Older Brother"). He is one of India's well-acclaimed social activists. Extensive media coverage and social networking websites have hailed Anna Hazare as the 'Gandhi of the 21st century.' This 75+ year old man has given a new hope to the young, modern India to fight to finish corruption. By setting a glorious example of decentralized governance in his own hometown, Ralegan Siddhi, Anna has provided a path for the modern India to coalesce into a new national movement against corruption.

Anna has been an instrumental figure in the Right to Information movement. In the early 2000s, Anna led a movement in the state of Maharashtra which forced the State Government to enact a revised Maharashtra Right to Information Act. This Act was later considered as the base document for the Right to Information Act 2005 enacted by the Central Government. Anna Hazare has always firmly believed that only when decentralization of power takes place the system will change. In order to bring change in the system, he feels that information should be made available to people regarding the government's actions and decisions. His persistent efforts through non-violent means brought pressure on the government, and both the Central and State Governments have enacted the Right to Information Act.

Anna through his 'Bhrashtachar Virodhi Jan Andolan' (People's Movement Against Corruption) movement has been spearheading the cause of eliminating corruption from day to day life and bringing about good governance. Through his movement, he wants to build national character, build an egalitarian society and create empowered citizenry.

In 2011, Anna initiated a Satyagraha (satya means truth and agraha means insistence; loosely translated as "truth force" or "insistence on truth" or "soul force") movement to pressurize the Indian Government for passing a stronger anti-corruption Lokpal (ombudsman) bill in the Indian Parliament as conceived in the Jan Lokpal Bill (People's Ombudsman Bill). This bill, also referred to as the Citizen's Ombudsman Bill, is an anti-corruption bill drafted and drawn up by prominent civil society activists, seeking the appointment of a Jan Lokpal. Jan Lokpal refers to an independent body to investigate corruption cases, address citizen grievances and provide protection to whistleblowers without government permission. The prefix "Jan" refers to citizens and their inputs through an activist-driven, non-governmental public consultation in improving this bill. The bill proposes institutions of the office of Lokpal at the center and Lok Ayukta at the state level. On the one hand, several Indians believe that India already has anti-corruption bureaucrats who have failed to solve this problem, and introducing the Jan Lokpal would be yet another huge bureaucratic failure, whereas on the other hand, there is a large chunk of the population that is ready to follow Anna Hazare to the ends of the world.

6.2.2 Arvind Kejriwal—An Icon of Emergent Leadership

Arvind Kejriwal is an Indian politician, former civil servant (Indian Revenue Service department) and an anti-corruption activist. In 2012, he moved away from Team Anna and founded the Aam Aadmi Party (AAP). AAP is an outcome of a mass movement in favor of a strong anti-corruption legislation, Jan

Lokpal; AAP has its roots in India's anti-corruption movement. Kejriwal contested and won the 2013 Delhi Legislative Assembly election, but his victory was short-lived—lasted only for 49 days. In the 2015 Delhi Legislative Assembly election, he won by a thumping majority and is now poised to take on the role of the Chief Minister. From the fiery speeches to the aam aadmi (common man) image that he projects, Kejriwal always stands out as a staunch exponent of anti-corruption. He shared the stage with Anna Hazare and participated in the mass movement for passing of the Jan Lokpal Bill. He played an instrumental role in campaigning to have the Central RTI Act passed.

During his 49-day tenure as Chief Minister, Kejriwal had launched a helpline that would help the common man combat corruption in Delhi. Addressing a gathering at Ramlila Maidan soon after taking oath as Chief Minister, he said during his tenure, the AAP Government had launched an anti-corruption helpline, which they will restart. Kejriwal has stated that he has entered politics with an aim to change the current corrupt and self-serving system. He has pledged to make Delhi the country's first corruption-free state.

Kejriwal has been awarded the Ramon Magsaysay Award for Emergent Leadership recognizing his social work, for activating the RTI movement at the grassroots and for his involvement in initiatives to fight corruption like the Parivartan movement (Parivartan means "change"). In 2006, Kejriwal had set up Public Cause Research Foundation (PCRF) to ensure accountable, just, transparent and participatory governance by focusing on two key areas of RTI and local self-governance. Kejriwal donated the prize money he had received from the Ramon Magsaysay Award to PCRF as a seed fund.

Will Kejriwal set a new gold standard of transparent governance? Will Kejriwal as the new Chief Minister rise above the limelight to become a beacon of anti-corruption in the political arena? Only time will reveal the answers to these questions. But the common man of Delhi has confidence that this young political organization led by an anti-corruption crusader will relieve them from the clutches of corruption to a considerable extent.

His anti-corruption goals, speeches, rallies and mandate have clearly struck a nerve with the nation in general and a major cross-section of Delhi's population in particular. The courage with which he has taken on powerful people has won Kejriwal a huge following. He has been termed as a maverick warrior against corruption.

6.2.3 *Satyendra Dubey—Lived for Truth, Died for Truth*

Satyendra Dubey was a project manager at the National Highways Authority of India. He wrote in a letter to the then Prime Minister of India, "A dream project of unparalleled importance to the nation, but in reality a great loot of public money because of very poor implementation at every state." He was killed after he blew the whistle on irregularities and flouting of rules in the Golden Quadrilateral highway construction project; a government project that he was working on, which aimed to connect many of the major cities.

This whistleblower said "don't name me" as he was risking his life by taking up a fight against the powerful construction mafia involved in the project. But just the opposite happened. His letter was leaked. He was shot dead in Gaya, Bihar. He exposed all the irregularities, right from the process of procurement to the quality of construction, but at the cost of exposing his identity and paying a big price—his own life. His death had sparked protests across the length and breadth of the country amidst calls for a legislation to protect the whistleblowers. All across the nation public meetings were held to protest against the death of Satyendra and to honour his courage. He was awarded several honours and medals posthumously. For honest citizens who want to follow in his footsteps, more than these honors, they want his sacrifice and the values that he upheld to be honored by giving him and his family justice. His sacrifice was completely dishonored when the judicial system and investigation agency declared that he died while fighting three robbers—yet another cover-up by the authorities.

Questions like did Satyendra die for nothing, why his request for secrecy was ignored, and why has there never been an open investigation of the alleged corruption within the NHAI, still haunt honest Indian minds. The name Satyendra means 'Lord of Truth.' Isn't it ironical that Satyendra lost his life for telling the truth? The only way to erase such haunting questions is to bring the real culprits to book irrespective how powerful they may be or politically influential they may be. His sacrifice will not amount to much unless we uphold the principles for which he gave up his life.

6.2.4 *Kiran Bedi—A Beacon of Integrity*

Kiran Bedi, India's first female police officer (now retired), is not only a staunch and well-known IPS (IPS stands for the Indian Police Service) officer but also a hard-core anti-corruption campaigner. She is one of the prominent members of the India Against Corruption (IAC) movement. Kiran Bedi was awarded the coveted Ramon Magsaysay Award in 1994 for government service. She is also responsible for establishing two voluntary organizations: Navjyoti in 1988 and India Vision Foundation in 1994. Both these organizations are about enhancing the quality of community services in various fields like education, rural development, crime prevention, women empowerment, etc.

According to Kiran Bedi, anti-corruption movements need to come together to form a coalition against corruption. If this nation is to get its Central Bureau of Investigation independent of the party in power then all different voices which have been speaking up need to come together in this cause and rise above ideologies and formations. She also wants women to be in the forefront of anti-corruption protests.

Kiran Bedi believes in the power of humanizing and reforming systems, right from the self to the prison system and from the government to the citizenry. Kiran Bedi is always on the move, promoting the religion of reform, publishing books on anti-corruption movements and crusaders, and delivering keynote lectures on anti-corruption across the globe.

Though Kiran Bedi was marred by controversies in recent times, yet she is considered as a beacon of integrity for the millions of Indians across the globe.

6.2.5 *Manjunath Shanmugam—Young India's Moral Compass*

Manjunath Shanmugam was a marketing manager for the Indian Oil Corporation who was killed for sealing corrupt petrol stations involved in oil adulteration in the Lakhimpur Kheri region in the state of Uttar Pradesh. This daring whistleblower became a victim of the very system he was trying to protect. Just like Satyendra Dubey, Manjunath Shanmugam was killed while fighting against corruption. During one of his surprise visits to see whether the ban was being executed, Manjunath was killed by a petrol pump owner and his accomplices in 2005. Even several years after this unfortunate event, as of May 2012, the case is pending before the Supreme Court.

The Manjunath Shanmugam Trust, an international pan-IIM alumni initiative, was established with a two-fold objective. The immediate objective is that of fighting the case, and the second objective includes a broader agenda of improving governance in Indian public life. The Trust also used to run India's first National Right to Information Act Helpline. Now it uses its funds to help local RTI activists.

Manjunath had exposed severe corruption in the multi-crore petroleum sector but nothing happened in this regards—there has been no change in the system. The only true way of honoring his sacrifice is to fight for his cause. By bringing pressure on the stakeholders involved in the system like the politicians and the companies to do away with the pricing anomaly and the rotten pricing system is the only lasting way of honoring Manjunath's heroic efforts.

Even till this day, the Indian youth honor his memory and the principles he stood for. The Manjunath Shanmugam Integrity Award honors and encourages those working to uphold the values of truth and honesty in Indian corporate, government or public life. The legacy of Manjunath has gone beyond the IIM community (IIM stands for the Indian Institutes of Management—a group of autonomous institutes of management education in India) to become an inspiration for the whole of India. He was born in Kolar, the land of golden soil, and indeed his sincere act proved that Manjunath was the purest gold culled from the mines of Kolar.

> **Spotlight**
>
> Cross currents of agendas within the social activism and civil society circle need to be eliminated as they are not a good sign for the overall anti-corruption movement.

Along with the above anti-corruption crusaders, there are several other known and celebrated heroes and unknown and unsung heroes, who are fighting for all of us against the growing menace of corruption in different parts of the nation. They are the torchbearers who motivate us to stand against corruption, instead of taking the easy way out. On the one hand, the Indian voters may seem to have accepted corruption as a fact of life, whereas on the other hand, the crusaders have sparked a widespread disillusionment at another level—the crusaders themselves get into an agenda mismatch at times. To clear this disillusionment, there need to be more crusaders within the system also (like economists, politicians, civil servants, legal experts, business leaders, police officers), who will support these external sources of anti-corruption to build a bias-free force to be reckoned with and that which will have direct engagement with its citizens. All the voices fighting their separate fights need to come together to form a solid coalition against corruption; they need to go beyond merely fasting, public meetings, marching and shouting slogans. Disillusionment in terms of agenda can only be eliminated when the anti-corruption crusaders keep away their personal agendas, do not indulge in dirty politics, stay away from glitz and glamour, and maintain laser-sharp focus on getting rid of governance deficit—only then followers of such crusaders will embrace and enhance the power of the civil society—only then the citizens will be able to identify with and offer support to true civil and social leadership. The Indian citizens need to seek answers to major questions like "do we need parallel bureaucracy to solve the issue of corruption?", "is rampant corruption a product of lack of implementation of existing laws and due to lack of laws?" and "are more anti-corruption movements required?" Finally, instead of idolizing or vilifying the icons of anti-corruption movements, the citizens of India should use their critical thinking skills to judge the merit of any anti-corruption movement before lending their voice and support to it.

6.3 Questions for Reflection

A. How can governments ensure access to human rights and justice?

B. Are the brutal deaths of anti-corruption crusaders worth the cause they were fighting for?

C. How can the business world foster civic leadership?

D. What qualities and abilities are needed to be an honest, hard-core whistleblower?

E. Why are anti-corruption crusades such as those led by social activist Anna Hazare gaining so much traction?

F. What are the advantages and disadvantages of the Jan Lokpal Bill?

G. How to encourage citizen participation in the process of anti-corruption policy making?

H. What can be done to bring the various anti-corruption crusaders and movements together under one roof?

7

The Indian Anti-Corruption Agenda—Closing Gaps Between Dreaming and Doing

In India making laws is not the real issue. The underlying question is how far these laws that are meant for the well-being of the citizens are implemented in spirit and word. Are they being implemented without any biases and prejudices? This chapter seeks to answer these questions and many more.

In the recent past, a string of corruption scandals such as Commonwealth Games and 2G Spectrum, has helped to rekindle a sense of intellectual independence and instilled a renewed vigor to fight against corruption within the people. This awakening of a new people power is dealt with in this chapter. We will talk about how the various abortive attempts to frame strong anti-corruption movements and discuss how these failures from the governance's end has given rise to a new crop of popular movements.

For any anti-corruption movement to be able to make an indelible impact through the power of oneness, it should first succeed in raising the awareness level about corruption and in mobilizing political will for reform. We will discuss how this dual purpose can be achieved by throwing light on the role of vigilance commissions, judicial activism, investigative journalism, etc. We will delve into the dynamics of various anti-corruption movements. The 2011 Indian anti-corruption movement is a strong case of non-violent rallies, mass protests and reasonable pressure on government. Organizations and movements like the

5th Pillar, Jaago Re! One Billion Votes, etc., are covered in this chapter too.

7.1 The New Wave of United Consciousness—Connecting Agents of Change

The recent wave of anti-corruption protests in India reflects the worry among Indians over the country's corruption menace. The 2011 uproar against corruption has not only rekindled academic interest on the issue of corruption, but has also motivated tens of thousands of Indians belonging to the middle-class to join in the protests—the rise of people power—connecting the agents of change. The uproar also stirred neighboring countries like Pakistan and also awakened the sleeping consciousness of Indians settled abroad in countries like the United Kingdom.

The bribe givers and the bribe takers are both from our own society. Only when we act as responsible citizens and become willing to change our attitudes and live by the morals of truth and integrity, we will be able to reconstruct a corruption-free society with an enhanced level of public accountability. It is all about minimizing conflicts of interests and maximizing the common good through reforms in all fields and at all levels.

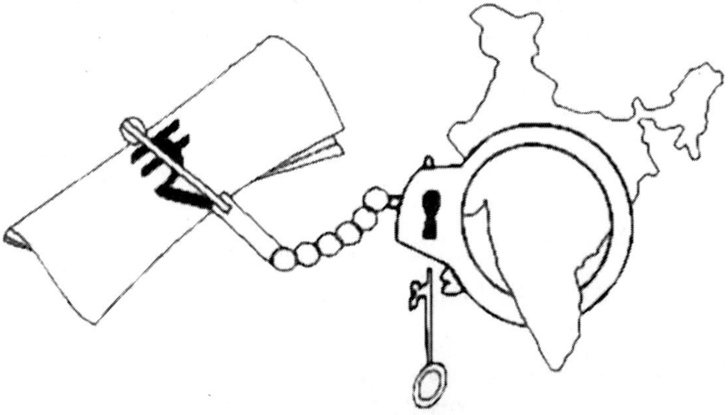

REFORMS

Illustration 7.1: The Key of Reforms

The agenda for action needs to include various reforms, aspects and mechanisms like tools for engaging citizens, strengthening of RTI as an instrument for enhancing government transparency, strengthening of political will and political culture, participatory performance monitoring, focus groups for supporting the citizen voice, etc.

Answers to relevant questions like to what extent are governmental and non-governmental factions aware of each other and how far do they cooperate towards the common goal of curbing corruption are addressed to fill in the gaps. New anti-corruption setups are discussed too. Virtualization of anti-corruption strategies through online systems and databases are the new ways of curbing corruption; they facilitate the sharing of data amongst anti-corruption agencies in real-time. These new setups are used for maintaining databases of corruption complaints, which can serve as a clearing house by referring the complaints to appropriate bodies. How the use of information technology in e-governance initiatives is helpful in reducing the corruption level and in giving a platform for public appeal is discussed. Several action points and reforms, right from reforming the political processes to social empowerment are discussed too.

Food for Thought

Rank and attribute a reason for the ranking of the following parameters that are needed to have a clean setup in any field:

A. Accountability
B. Responsibilities of the Stakeholders
C. Transparency
D. Training and Education
E. Resources
F. Working Conditions

7.1.1 *A New Political Culture—Commitment to the Society*

Eradicating corruption requires a new political culture in India. The Global Integrity 2008 Report shows that government initiatives to control corruption at the institutional level face a big implementation gap in terms of policy adoption and policy outcome. They are either poorly implemented or remain on paper. Transparency International has continually cited the lack of political will to enforce and implement anti-corruption measures.

Spotlight

Political culture and political will are integral catalysts in curbing the abuse of power.

In a democratic setup like India, only when both creation and implementation of laws is achieved, will a new political culture be achieved. Not mere adoption of laws in the Parliament will close the implementation gaps. Only when the government adopts laws and implements them too, the people will be able to place their trust in the political will of their leaders. Political will refers to the high-level advocacy and credible intent of a government to implement stringent laws, including anti-corruption laws, for the benefit of the society. Political will also refers to the capacity to effectively carry out duties assigned to political leaders.

A strong political will at all levels of the Indian Government can be achieved through societal reforms and institutional reforms. Before implementing such reforms, an assessment of the reform opponents and supporters and their demands and interests needs to be done. Assessment of other factors like how much support has the Indian Government provided in terms of legal support, training in corruption prevention, internal audits, ethical conduct, anti-corruption budget and leadership by example. Such in-depth analysis is needed to identify priority areas to introduce corruption prevention reforms.

At times, even if there is an appropriate political culture and political will, there could be a lack of experience and education among government officials, or there is a lack of material resources, or there could be opposition from certain stakeholders. The solution for overcoming these hurdles is training, intra-governmental communication, engagement of all stakeholders, and realistic goals and reforms. Open dialog with all stakeholders, including the public, helps to establish a trust-worthy political culture and political will. No group or institution should feel isolated. These aspects will help to create public trust in the anti-corruptions reforms and laws.

There needs to be an elaborate check and balance system to prevent the abuse of the discretionary powers of the political setup. While political will in the Indian political setup may be spread unevenly across the setup, it is important to identify leaders with a strong political will to use their dedication for developing the required depth and reach of political will. A committed political culture and a strong political will are needed in India in order to institutionalize and sustain anti-corruption reforms and changes. The political actors need to back their words with actions. Without a committed political will, the anti-corruption efforts and campaigns by other stakeholders of the society remain mere rhetoric.

7.1.2 *Judiciary Integrity—Fair and Vigilant Justice*

Many people see police, lawyers, court officials and judges as a source of unfair and corrupt practices. A fair and vigilant judiciary is the key to successful anti-corruption initiatives. A multi-thronged, holistic approach towards achieving judicial integrity, accountability and transparency is necessary.

The first stage of judicial corruption begins with the police department. Tackling and uprooting corruption from the police forces is critical for preventing corruption from seeping in to the higher-up levels. For tackling police corruption, one of the most important steps is to ensure that complaints against the police are dealt with by a truly independent body. But this independent body will be a success only when it is backed by unwavering public support. The separation of law and order staff and crime investigation units at the police station level in urban areas was ordered by a Supreme Court judgment in 2006, however, this has been only partially implemented in many Indian states. Another factor that will help to minimize corruption at police stations is that they should be given adequate petty cash to meet day-to-day expenditure. Mere transfer or suspension of corrupt police officials won't work. Concrete steps like dismissal from service, police case or exemplary punishment will deter other officers from indulging in corrupt acts.

Judicial and legal bodies like law societies and bar associations need to be more vigilant. Apart from reporting cases and instances of corruption in the system, these bodies should also show their willingness and responsibility towards the effective implementation of measures to instill moral discipline in the professionals of this field.

The Bangalore Principles on judicial conduct is a most comprehensive guide of international standards on judicial conduct. These principles advocate six core principles of independence, impartiality, integrity, propriety, equality and finally competence and diligence in order to ensure fair investigation and ethical conduct.

The government should facilitate the court system to fast-track all cases of corruption, nepotism and moral turpitude. The process of impeachment of corrupt judges should be speeded up with a time limit for obtaining the President's sanction and impeaching culprit judges.

Adequate resources and protection measures in terms of better salaries, better working conditions, safety, training, etc., should be available to the judicial system so as to enable the judiciary to carry out its responsibilities effectively.

Computerization of court work will aid in reducing the work load, reducing duplication of work, listing the different stages of judicial files/cases, and in speeding up administration of justice. The concept of e-driven information help desk needs to be implemented across the system to guide people through the judicial procedures.

To increase and deepen public awareness of disciplinary processes, court procedures, prosecution guidelines, practices, proposed changes, etc., bulletins need to be produced and disseminated. Even independent watchdog committees can be set up that can disseminate information to civil society organizations and the public. Public access to this information provides a means of challenging irregularities. These committees can also act as a watchdog to ensure fair trials. The academia (NGOs, civil society, citizens, associations, legal experts) should contribute to the understanding of issues related to judicial corruption and offer their expert advice to judicial reform programmes.

The role of media and investigative journalism in enhancing judicial integrity should not be limited to undercover informants, sting operations, wide coverage of scams, etc. Media professionals and journalists need to be trained in accurate court reporting, investigative techniques and fair commenting as it is essential for building pressure on the judicial system to grant justice to victims of corruption. This training is necessary so that the media does not sensationalize issues and indulge in malicious criticism, and instead presents fair and sensible accounts of what is happening in the judicial setup. Training workshops also cultivate and increase the media's commitment to fight corruption, including judicial corruption.

Judicial integrity is an amalgamation of various factors—both individual independence and institutional independence ensure that the judicial office is not abused and the judicial officials give out reasoned judgments purely on the basis of facts and evidence. There should be no scope for interference from interest groups and political parties. Clear administrative accountability and processes in terms of merit-based selection of judges, objective case assignment, misconduct and removal of judicial officials, etc., should be in place. Conflicts of interests should be avoided. Judges must declare conflicts of interests as soon as they become apparent. The executive and legislature wings must not influence the appeals process or judicial outcomes. These wings should not remove or transfer judges for personal or political reasons. Judicial officials need to educate themselves continuously in various areas of their work like legal developments, ethics, best practices and anti-corruption laws.

7.1.3 *Corporate Social Responsibility and Governance—Trust-Building is the Key*

India has been touted as a future global economic giant. Although India is poised for great economic growth, there is one problem seeping through the corporate world—corruption. The National Foundation for Corporate Governance was set up by the Ministry of Corporate Affairs to promote better corporate governance practices, ethics and processes in India. The Ministry of Corporate Affairs has also issued the National Voluntary Guidelines on Social, Environmental and Economic Responsibilities of Business and the Voluntary Guidelines for Corporate Governance. These guidelines are concrete measures for companies to safeguard the interests of the shareholders, investors, employees, customers, environment and the society.

These guidelines include principles like ethics, transparency and accountability, respect of human rights, value addition to the society, equitable growth and restoration of the environment.

The Companies Bill passed by the Lok Sabha in 2012 has introduced certain new concepts, including that of Corporate Social Responsibility (CSR). This bill seeks to make CSR spending compulsory for companies that meet certain criteria. Indian companies and organizations should build and maintain a laser-sharp focus on the goals of corporate social responsibility. By doing so, they can make the society and stakeholders, including employees and customers, feel confident about their agenda. A happy customer is a repeat customer, and will continuously add to the profits. If a customer feels exploited or society questions an organization's integrity, there will be negative impact on an organization's image.

Organizations need to implement the Global Compact Principle 10—"Businesses should work against corruption in all its forms, including extortion and bribery."

According to a popular definition, corporate governance is "the system by which companies are directed and controlled" (Cadbury Committee, 1992). A wider and deeper meaning is given by India's SEBI Committee on Corporate Governance. The committee defines corporate governance as the "acceptance by management of the inalienable rights of shareholders as the true owners of the corporation and of their own role as trustees on behalf of the shareholders. It is about commitment to values, about ethical business conduct and about making a distinction between personal and corporate funds in the management of a company."

Better corporate governance helps to reduce corrupt practices. It facilitates trust-building within the shareholders, investors and the general public as these stakeholders get a transparent picture of the financial flows and business transactions. Indian corporate bodies and organizations need to demonstrate all the stated responsibilities through their actions and policies.

7.1.4 *Citizen Voice—Strengthening People Participation*

Person A paid 1550 rupees for passport processing. Person B paid a heavy sum for obtaining a building completion certificate.

These are the commonplace corruption experiences experienced by Indians. Mere anti-corruption policies or integrity workshops are not enough for mobilizing public opinion against such corruption scenarios. A well-informed citizenry, a clean social mindset and unwavering commitment to act as a responsible citizen are needed to improve transparency and accountability at all levels of the society. To sustain these aspects, a diagnostic and research outlook is needed to not only identify corruption-related risks and problems, but also to work out an effective agenda of constructive initiatives to counter corruption.

There needs to be an increasing direct contact between government and citizens. Fighting corruption is not the responsibility of only government machinery but also of the citizens. Ethics and values need to be instilled right from a young age through youth education and ethics development, corruption prevention seminars, etc.

Spotlight

Indian citizens should build pressure at all levels of the government machinery to allow them unrestricted access to information and to include them in auditing government processes and projects.

Public access to official outcomes and information is necessary for citizens to be well-informed, and only well-informed citizens can stand up for their rights and fight out till the end. The level of information access also determines the effectiveness of corrective actions.

Organized protests, social accountability initiatives, public relations campaigns, focus groups, surveys, capacity building initiatives, institutional oversight bodies, and participatory performance monitoring tools like social audits are needed for supporting the citizen voice and activating all nodes of citizen involvement, which in turn will help to promote good governance processes, prevent leakage of public funds and hold the policymakers accountable for their commitments and decisions. The citizens of India need to play a more active role in the policy developments and decisions that affect them in order to link "citizen voice" and "transparency, accountability and responsiveness." Community participation in government-funded projects leads to better budget transparency and project outcomes.

A free and vigilant press and media can help to galvanize the citizen voice and public opinion on matters related to public service performance, public expenditures, etc., thereby helping to transform concerned individuals into engaged and empowered citizens. Empirical research shows that corruption is lower in countries where the press is free.

Decentralization helps to bridge the gaps between the government and its voters. It provides an opportunity for the ordinary citizens to influence the development and implementation of policies and laws at various levels of the government. Moreover, citizens need to be given the mechanism and right to demand a formal investigation against government irregularities.

All these aspects will work only when there is equal representation of all factions of society. Control by a particular class or interest group such as the elites will lead to further marginalization of the deprived or poor sections of the society. Again the lack of resources, lack of access to information and low awareness of rights will not produce the desired effects. These flaws need to be addressed first in order to have the citizen voice heard and acted upon through concrete techniques.

7.1.5 *E-Governance—Transparent Governance*

A range of public services like filing tax returns, obtaining licences, etc., have been digitized in India to a certain extent. E-governance and computerized procedures have helped to reduce the influence of middle men, considerably—but there is still a long way to go. It has helped to reduce human intervention and the exercise of discretionary powers, especially in all those services which are vulnerable to corruption—but Zero Corruption is still a distant dream.

The Central Vigilance Commission adopted the strategy of "Leveraging Technology to Prevent Corruption" since 2004, wherein organizations are persuaded to adopt e-governance. Through this strategy, CVC is committed to not only simplifying processes but also using information technology for empowering all the stakeholders in the fight against corruption. The National Portal of India—this portal has been developed as a Mission Mode Project (MMP) under the National E-Governance Plan (NEGP) of the government. Its main aim is to support the growth of e-governance within the country and to provide a single window access to the information and services being provided by the Indian Government. The National Informatics Center (NIC) is a premier science and technology organization, which has spearheaded the e-governance drive with an aim to establish transparent governance. NIC has developed and implemented a large number of e-governance applications for the Central Government, State Governments and other bodies. Some of the e-governance projects by NIC are Samvad Software (Web-based Complaint Monitoring System), COIN (Co-Operative Banking in Place), Project Monitoring and Information System (PMIS), Consumer Forum Computerization (CONFONET), etc. India needs to have more and more such initiatives and projects in order to introduce predictability in the functioning of the government departments.

India also needs to tap into the social media space by leveraging the power of social media tools and technology to enable efficient government management and to fight corruption. Social media options like blogs, micro-blogging services, social networking sites, etc., can be used to collaborate and empower citizens and the other factions of society through social interaction and address issues, including corruption, in real-time.

Nation-wide adoption of e-governance and ICT tools will not only reduce paperwork and arbitrariness, and help to synchronize the functioning of the various departments, but also provide services and information to citizens and businesses at the click of the mouse, which in turn will help to follow-up on actions and trace decisions. For example, information in the form of application forms or actual delivery of services like filing tax returns. E-governance leaves little room for bribes and administrative corruption, and this objective can be achieved only when all types of data and information is made transparent, right from rules and procedures to performance indicators and from decisions of the government to the outcomes of these decisions.

A Word of Caution

Complete e-enabling is a lengthy and difficult process due to several gaps.

Complete e-enabling is a lengthy and difficult process due to several gaps like the lack of a comprehensive e-strategy, lack of technology literacy and weak technological infrastructure. Central-state and inter-state cooperation, legal infrastructure to accommodate the current and future technology, technical framework in terms of connectivity, hardware and software, e-literacy of people and institutional capacity are necessary to popularize and stabilize e-governance. Another gap that needs to be considered while designing a foolproof e-governance strategy is that the new-age government officials and civil servants who are tech-savvy can use their knowledge to bypass checkpoints in e-governance. The Government along with inputs from experts in the fields of policymaking and technology need to adopt a strategy of pilot projects, wherein small-scale e-projects are implemented in departments to identify and correct any technical and non-technical gaps.

7.2 Novel Initiatives—One Step Further

Though there are a lot of anti-corruption bills, agencies and initiatives in India, yet due to political interference, they are not able to achieve their anti-corruption goals as expected. According to Global Integrity and Transparency International, the institutional setup suffers from the lack of coordination between the different stakeholders. Moreover, although public participation and civil society involvement is increasing, yet it is still not enough to bring about autonomy in the various anti-corruption efforts. Other supportive factors like realistic goals, citizen centricity, careful planning, service orientation and an all-inclusive strategy need to be fine-tuned. The unsuccessful attempts to frame strong anti-corruption movements and failures from the governance's end are major causes for the rise of civil society-based initiatives and business coalitions to fight against the menace of corruption. Governance failures have led businesses to mitigate corrupt business to business transactions with an aim to deal with corruption at the business to government level too.

There are several e-governance initiatives undertaken at various Central and State Government ministries. The Gyandhoot project launched in Madhya Pradesh is a community-owned rural intranet system that caters to the needs of the village community through a series of kiosks. Drishtee is a multi-state project aimed to be the 'window to the world' for Indian villagers. Through its network of kiosks and a tiered franchise and partnership model, Drishtee provides not only cost-effective access to information and services like health and education, but also generates employment opportunities for the unemployed rural population. Computer-aided Administration of Registration Department (CARD) is an e-governance initiative in Andhra Pradesh. The main objective of CARD is to minimize corruption in the registration procedure. Lokvani is an e-governance initiative in Uttar Pradesh, which provides the public with more efficient and effective means of reporting problems to the government.

The Pahal ("beginning") programme has made villagers more aware of their rights. Its main aim is to encourage villagers to participate in local processes and administration.

The ipaidabribe.com is a unique initiative by Janaagraha (Janaagraha is a non-profit organization, which focuses on improving the quality of life in Indian towns and cities, facilitating direct accountability of the government to the people, and enabling and empowering citizens and local governments), which aims at curbing corruption by harnessing the collective power of the citizens. The website has become a major platform where people can share experiences related to corruption of any form. This website provides reports on bribe trends, stories on bribes and corruption, a repository of corruption-related data across government departments, etc. This website has led to the emergence of similar websites in China.

Certain anti-corruption organizations like the Lok Satta Movement have transformed itself from a civil organization to a full-fledged political party, the Lok Satta Party. The Lok Satta Movement is a non-partisan movement for democratic reforms started in 1996. It operates based on principle of 'democracy is for the people, of the people and by the people.' This movement transformed into the Lok Satta Party in 2006. Its goals focus on self-governance, self-correcting institutional mechanisms, empowerment of citizens, freedom and rule of law. The party intends to further these causes of the Lok Satta Movement.

Karmayog provides a networking hub for NGOs and citizens to engage with each other, and with the media, government and institutions. It strongly believes that citizen focus and participation is needed to solve civic and social issues. It provides a resource base containing an all India NGOs directory and information on civic and social issues.

5th Pillar of India is a non-profit organization known for creating the zero-rupee note containing anti-corruption slogans. The purpose of this is to instill confidence in people to say no to bribery. These notes can be used to pay government officials who solicit bribes in return for services which are supposed to be free. This concept of using valueless fantasy currency against corruption has been adopted by nations like Nepal and Mexico too.

Jaago Re! One Billion Votes is an extension of Tata Tea's Jaago Re! Campaign. Jaago Re! One Billion Votes is a joint initiative by Janaagraha and Tata Tea. Its main aim is to encourage citizens, especially the youth, to cast their votes to influence the elections and political agenda so as to transition India into a better nation.

There needs to be cooperation and cross-pollination of knowledge and ideas between such organizations, initiatives, movements and campaigns. There needs to be coordination between corruption prevention and investigation agencies and authorities. More and more such novel initiatives are needed to heighten the awareness level of citizens and to help them recognize and deal with scenarios of corruption.

7.3 Questions for Reflection

A. What are the cultural and systemic challenges facing anti-corruption compliance in India?

B. In what ways can politicians be tempted to (ab)use their positions in order to obstruct the process of reforms?

C. Who do you think would be likely to oppose anti-corruption reforms? And what would be their motives?

D. How well do you think the anti-corruption agencies perform in terms of their agenda and goals?

E. Should anti-corruption become one of the key objectives of the e-governance vision?

F. What is the relationship between good governance and anti-corruption?

PART 4

Beyond Boundaries—We Need More Role Models

8

Cross-Country Analysis and Efforts—Lessons Learned

In this chapter, we compare India's anti-corruption efforts and experiences of combating corruption with other nations like that of the United States, Malaysia, Hong Kong, etc. A cross-country analysis will help us to pinpoint options for reforms that have worked in other nations and can also be applied to the Indian situation as well. Several major sources of data like Transparency International's Corruption Indices, Gallup's Opinion Surveys, etc., are included to shed light on the damaging effects of corruption worldwide, global dynamics of corruption and many more aspects.

As I stated earlier, the key to minimizing corruption is disabling its causes, both at the national and global levels. In the earlier sections, we have discussed the local aspect related to the Indian subcontinent and here we will cover how the international community is curbing corruption through various conventions, bodies, certificates, pacts, etc., and also how India is supporting these global efforts.

Hard data and evidence of corruption is difficult to obtain because of the secrecy associated with it and also the results can be subjectively affected due to cultural influences. But still there are organizations working relentlessly to present empirical and objective findings. Earlier, corruption was analyzed from a country-specific viewpoint, but now it is analyzed using cross-country data as corruption operates on a global scale. Many global organizations like the World Bank, UN Convention Against Corruption, Transparency International, etc., are working hard to present data by going beyond mere perception-based rankings, which can be a key to finding other sources of corruption. They carry out various initiatives to fight corruption in all of its forms. These organizations and agencies are doing all they can do to give a comparative analysis of corruption using various determinants of corruption like real per capita GDP, unemployment rate, etc., to explain differences in corruption across nations.

Transparency International's Global Corruption Barometer is the largest cross-country survey to collect the general public's views on corruption in their countries. Global Integrity provides reports, data and scorecards on factors like corruption trends and corruption challenges around the world. The World Bank publishes aggregate and individual governance indicators for numerous countries and territories, which contribute to the growing empirical research of governance levels across countries.

8.1 Cross-Country Cleanups—The Role of Global Organizations

No country is entirely free of corruption. Although the effects and forms of corruption vary from country to country, they do share common roots. A cross-country analysis will give us a holistic sense of where does India stand in terms of its own anti-corruption strategies, both on a local and worldwide levels.

On the one hand, the public perception of the various aspects of corruption and its effects have been gathered and studied through various surveys carried out across the world, and on the other hand, several anti-corruption activities by bilateral and multilateral institutions is on the rise.

For implementing effective local and cross-country corruption cleanups, measuring corruption on all levels is of utmost importance. Only then reforms can be implemented successfully. Only then corruption areas can be prioritized and the fabric of the world society can be restored. It is important to note that several organizations conduct surveys related to the various aspects of corruption, but merely conducting surveys is not enough. The findings and results of the surveys need to be published in order to increase public awareness.

Transparency International publishes several indices that measure the prevalence of corruption globally. For example, the Corruption Perceptions Index (CPI) is a composite index that ranks nations according to their perceived level of corruption. CPI ranks countries on a scale from 0 (highly corrupt) to 10 (very clean). Another important index is the Bribe Payers Index, which ranks leading exporting nations according to the propensity of their companies to bribe to win business abroad. This index reveals the 'supply side' of corruption and this index is based on the views of thousands of senior business executives from developed and developing nations. Gallup's opinion surveys (Gallup is a research-based performance-management consulting organization) are conducted in more than 140 nations. The survey results are published in the form of data-driven news about various social, political and economic issues, including corruption. Another index that is useful for cross-regional comparisons is the Control of Corruption Index (CCI) by the World Bank. CCI gathers data from a wider range of sources. Such findings and survey results are needed to build a database of quantitative and qualitative information, which can help in prioritizing institutional areas of corruption, in designing anti-corruption policies, and in identifying subjective and objective measures of corruption across regions and nations.

According to the Transparency International Corruption Report (2005), "seven out of ten countries score less than 5 out of a clean score of 10 and nine out of ten developing countries score less than 5 against a clean score of 10." Countries with higher corruption scores have a lower ratio of total and private investment to GDP, and, consequently, lower economic growth (Mauro, 1995). Nations that are home to illicit syndicates, mafia groups or outlaw enterprises can extend their corrupt clout to other countries in an attempt to protect and expand their illegal network. Weak nations in terms of political instability, small size, poverty, extent of decentralization, economic vulnerability, etc., can experience severe cross-border corruption, which in turn can lead to more domestic corruption—they feed on each other. Economic realities like multiple exchange rates, high cost of movement of goods and capital, etc., give rise to unofficial markets. Transparency International's bribe payers index finds that companies from India, Malaysia, China and Taiwan frequently pay high levels of bribes when conducting business overseas—often after their own natural resources have been exhausted. Nations plagued with cross-border corruption are not able to make the best use of their economic, natural and human resources as it affects domestic corruption too. All these facts show different figures and findings based on various determinants, but they also echo one common factor that corruption has both local and cross-border impact. Therefore, cross-border policies and strategies of reform need to be carefully integrated with domestic realities of corruption in order to minimize points of vulnerability that can cause cross-border corruption. A combination of observed data, perceptions and factors that may make nations vulnerable to corruption will help in measuring corruption more accurately.

Table 8.1: Some Popular Indices

Index	Purpose/Scope	Source
Bribe Payers Index (BPI)	BPI ranks leading exporting nations according to the propensity of their companies to bribe abroad. BPI captures the 'supply side' of corruption.	Transparency International
Corruption Perceptions Index (CPI)	CPI scores countries on how corrupt their public sectors are seen to be based on expert assessments and opinion surveys.	Transparency International
Global Integrity Index	The index measures the existence and effectiveness of laws and practices that prevent corruption. It measures the gap between the quality and implementation of anti-corruption laws.	Global Integrity
Control of Corruption Index (CCI)	CCI is an aggregation of various indicators that measure the degree to which corruption is perceived to exist among public officials, businesses and politicians. CCI measures the extent to which public power is exercised for private gain, including both petty and grand forms of corruption, as well as 'capture' of the state by elites and private interests.	World Bank

Anti-corruption initiatives are increasingly acquiring a global hue. The recent surge of interest for fighting corruption from all corners of the world is a good sign for the global anti-corruption campaign.

Here we will take a look at the role played by international cooperation agencies, networks, conference programs and collaborative solutions in combating corruption both in India and on a global level. Such organizations help to propagate good practices and new reforms to establish transparency. They provide the broad-based platform, resources, expertise and experience needed for combining and coordinating actions against corruption. All these aspects are described in this chapter.

8.1.1 *A Cooperative Approach—Globalized Corruption, Globalized Anti-Corruption Measures*

Corruption has existed from the beginning of time. Globalization has increased the magnitude of corruption and the opportunities for corruption. Corruption has now become increasingly organized and transnational. The ever-increasing "epidemic" of corruption in both developed and developing countries has led to more cooperation throughout the world community.

Corruption is not just an India-centric problem; it is a global problem. Nonetheless, a cooperative approach to curb corruption across nations is truly the need of the hour as agents of cross-border corruption are capable of doing business almost everywhere, but it is hard to hold them accountable anywhere. Just as each and every nation is globalized today, so is corruption. So why not globalize the measures to fight it too! This is where international organizations, treaties and initiatives come into play. Over the years, policymakers, anti-corruption initiatives, business entities, financial institutions, community leaders and civil society organizations in particular and the masses in general have come to appreciate how critical the role of international cooperation is for sustained reforms and to a better understanding of the cross-border aspects of corruption.

Citizen participation, both at the national and global levels is necessary to build a moral conscience. Government agencies, experts and NGOs from various countries are already conducting conferences and forming joint initiatives across the world to develop multidisciplinary approaches in order to create a good governance agenda and sustainable anti-corruption standards and safeguards against corruption.

A Word of Caution

The attitude of "chalta hain"—it means it is okay needs to be replaced with cooperative, collective action. Only then the international community can be successful in reducing poverty and increasing economic growth around the world.

As corruption is not only a moral or political issue, but also an economic problem, one of the major aims of international efforts is controlling corruption in international business. To maintain this focus, major international financial organizations like the regional development banks, the International Monetary Fund and the World Bank are playing a vigilant role by aligning anti-corruption reforms and efforts to the allocation of funds.

The World Bank initiatives like the Anti-Corruption Knowledge Resource Center and the World Bank Institute (WBI) provide strategic directions on improving the level of collaborative governance and combating corruption. The World Bank uses technological advances to keep a tab on corruption through its Integrity Vice Presidency (INT). INT was established in 2001 as the independent arm of the Bank responsible for ensuring the Bank's development resources and funds are not misused. INT plays a crucial role in the Bank-financed projects in terms of investigating collusions, violations of agreed standards, frauds, suspicious transactions, etc. The World Bank collaborates with multilateral development banks, international organizations and NGOs like the Transparency International. For example, the World Bank has collaborated with Transparency International in designing and delivering seminars related to anti-corruption strategies and programs.

The Organization of American States (OAS) is the first international legal framework that criminalized the bribery of foreign government officials. Its members are the 35 independent states of the United States of America. The main aims of OAS are promoting security, peace and cooperative action, and eliminating bribery and corruption of government officials.

Most countries have laws to deal with bribes involving domestic public officials. OECD Anti-Bribery Convention is a major step in reducing corruption in developing countries by encouraging sanctions against bribery in international business transactions carried out by companies based in the convention member countries. This convention aims at curbing bribes involving foreign public officials. Through its efforts, compliances and strategies, this convention sends out a clear signal that business will be done purely on the basis of sound economic judgment and not through underhand dealings.

The United Nations Development Programme (UNDP) is a major provider of anti-corruption technical support and advisory services to approximately 103 countries. UNDP has partnerships with other anti-corruption organizations like the Basel Institute on Governance, UN Office of Drugs and Crime, etc. Through various programs like the Global Programme on Anti-Corruption for Development Effectiveness (PACDE), UNDP helps countries to improve governance and reduce corruption.

The Food and Agriculture Organization of the United Nations (FAO) is a neutral forum which ensures that best practices are followed in order to ensure good nutrition levels and food security. FAO aims to eliminate corrupt practices in order to make sure that people have regular access to high-quality food.

Several knowledge-sharing portals have been created for raising awareness about global corruption. The Anti-Corruption Authorities (ACAs) Portal provides a platform for sharing ideas and experiences. More than 30 countries have established some type of Anti-corruption Authorities (ACAs), which help in policy coordination, public outreach, investigation, etc. The U4 Anti-Corruption Resource Centre (previously referred to as the Utstein Anti-Corruption Resource Centre) is a web-based resource centre for donor practitioners and development agencies to effectively address corruption challenges. It maintains web-based resource pages on various themes developed for a donor audience like corruption in the health sector, political corruption, etc. Tools and Resources for Anti-Corruption Knowledge (TRACK) is a centralized knowledge repository. TRACK was launched by UNODC in September 2011. TRACK is a web-based anti-corruption portal with an aim to provide a common platform of collaboration between anti-corruption practitioners, member states, experts and partner institutions.

The United States is a forerunner in the fight against corruption. This nation lays heavy stress on transparency and accountability. Through various initiatives like the Deauville Partnership and Open Government Partnership, the United States encourages civil society organizations, government leaders, citizens and countries to bring more transparency and accountability. Through the Deauville Partnership, the United States has committed itself to support ongoing efforts in the Middle East and North Africa to recover stolen assets and fight corruption.

Though the United States is a leader in anti-corruption enforcement, other nations like the United Kingdom and Australia are also focusing their efforts in strengthening anti-corruption laws and regulations. The United Kingdom brought into force its Bribery Act 2010 in July 2011. The Australian Government works closely with partner governments to support their own efforts to tackle corruption through the international development assistance program. Australia provides help to its partner governments in terms of training, strengthening of anti-corruption laws and reforms, curbing transnational organized crime and combating money laundering. Australia provides this aid through units and treaties like the Regional Legal Assistance Unit and the International Assistance and Treaties Branch. Turkey is another country that is strongly committed to anti-corruption. Turkey has also ratified the Council of Europe Civil and Criminal Law Conventions on Corruption. Turkey is among the first countries to have signed the UN Convention Against Corruption in December 2003. Hong Kong's fight against corruption over the years has proved a success model in terms of a strong political will, investigation, prevention and legislative support. Hong Kong's Independent Commission Against Corruption (ICAC) is one of the successful anti-corruption agencies in the world. Public education is an important part of ICAC through which it reaches out to people, especially the youth, through anti-corruption and moral education programmes. Malaysia is also performing a vigilant role through various agencies and initiatives, for example, the Malaysian Anti-Corruption Commission (MACC), which is modeled after top anti-corruption agencies like the Independent Commission Against Corruption (Australia) and Independent Commission Against Corruption (Hong Kong). It provides training modules in areas like prosecution, security, investigations, etc., and assists in building international relations in order to combat corruption.

The Building Integrity Initiative, established by the Euro-Atlantic Partnership Council in 2007, is open to all Allies and NATO's partners in the Euro-Atlantic area, the Mediterranean and the Gulf region, as well as other partners across the globe, including Afghanistan. This initiative aims in strengthening good governance, management and integrity within the defence and security sectors.

Revenue Watch International (RWI) is a non-profit policy institute and multi-stakeholder initiative that works with the civil society, media, policymakers and key organizations such as the World Bank, Transparency International and Oxfam in resource-dependent countries. RWI promotes accountable and transparent management of oil, gas and mineral resources for the public good.

Organizations like TRACE and Transparency International provide anti-bribery training, tools to diagnose, measure and fight corruption, research on various corruption topics and due diligence reports. Transparency International's Advocacy and Legal Advice Centers (ALACs) provide the victims of corruption with practical assistance to pursue their complaints against corruption.

Civil society organizations, industry associations and business houses too are putting in their share of contribution to create a deep-rooted anti-corruption culture. Several nations and their business communities have already set examples of transparent business operations by introducing integrity pacts and compliance pacts. Civil society organizations in turn help to make the public aware of such pacts. Civil society organizations also act as a watchdog over government, public sector and private sector anti-corruption efforts. NGOs like the Venezuela-based Agrupacion Pro Calidad de Vida organize nation-wide workshops to teach the Venezuelan citizens about how best to minimize corruption; similar efforts can be undertaken in the Indian subcontinent.

In 1990, only 13 countries had Right to Information (RTI) laws or policies of information disclosure, but by 2007 the number had gone up to 70. Several nations, including India, have recognized the importance of the RTI for protecting human rights and fundamental freedoms.

The private sector in various countries is making anti-corruption efforts through various organizations like the World Economic Forum's Partnering Against Corruption Initiative (PACI) and the Global Compact Anti-Corruption Principle (Principle 10). PACI is a global initiative developed by companies for companies. PACI helps companies to benchmark internal practices against global best practices, provides a platform to share peer knowledge and provides strategies to prevent, detect and deal with corruption. The Global Compact Anti-Corruption Principle is derived from the United Nations Convention Against Corruption. Its main aim is not only to curb bribery, extortion and other forms of corruption, but also to design policies and concrete programs to address corruption.

These conventions, laws, protocols, forums and pacts show that there are relentless efforts being made on a worldwide level to ensure that the rights of people are respected and protected. They clearly show a trend towards national legislations with an international reach.

Table 8.2: Conventions, Protocols and Action Plans Across the Globe

Region	Conventions, Protocols and Plans
Asia	ADB-OECD Anti-Corruption Action Plan for Asia-Pacific
Europe	Council of Europe Criminal Law Convention European Union Convention Against Corruption involving Officials

United States of America	Inter-American Convention Against Corruption (IACAC) Organization of American States
Africa	Economic Community of West African States Protocol on the Fight Against Corruption South African Development Protocol Against Corruption (SADC)

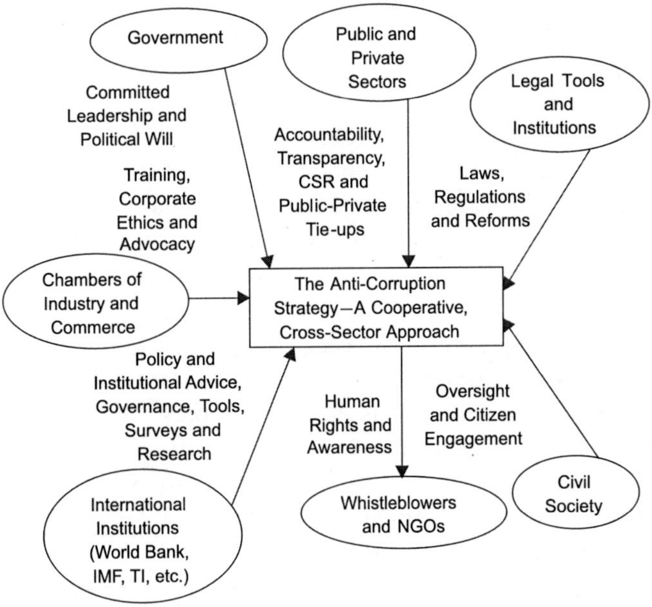

Figure 8.1: The Anti-Corruption Strategy—A Cooperative, Cross-Sector Approach

8.2 India's Role in the Global Efforts—Growing in Scope

In 2000, a group of senior judges from Asia and Africa met in Bangalore and listed a set of core principles, known as the Bangalore Principles of Judicial Conduct, in order to curb judicial corruption: independence, impartiality, integrity, propriety, equality and finally competence and diligence. The Bangalore Principles of Judicial Conduct have since then been endorsed by a number of international bodies like the United Nations

Commission on Human Rights in 2003 and the United Nations Commission on Crime Prevention and Criminal Justice in 2006.

In 2001, India joined the ADB-OECD Anti-Corruption initiative for Asia-Pacific, which is joint initiative by the Asian Development Bank (ADB) and the Organization for Economic Cooperation and Development (OECD). This initiative focuses on encouraging active public involvement, developing transparency and strengthening integrity in business operations.

In 2003, the first legally binding international anti-corruption instrument came into being—the United Nations Convention Against Corruption (UNCAC). UNCAC is a major step in promoting international cooperation against corruption. The member-countries are bound to provide mutual legal assistance in the prosecution of offenders as well as in tracing, freezing and confiscating the proceeds of corruption. India ratified the UNCAC in 2011.

India also ratified yet another UN Convention in 2011, the United Nations Convention Against Transnational Organized Crime (UNTOC). UNTOC is the first comprehensive and global legally binding instrument to fight transnational organized crime. There are several other legal frameworks like the Inter-American Convention Against Corruption, OECD Convention on Combating Bribery of Foreign Public Officials in International Business Transactions, etc., which are striving hard to establish robust anti-corruption standards on a global level.

In recent times, the Indians have become more aware of corruption at all levels all because of civil society activism. In 2011, the Hon. ex-President of India, Pratibha Patil, announced that India would soon join the International Anti-Corruption Academy (IACA) in Austria. IACA is a joint initiative by the United Nations Office on Drugs and Crime (UNODC), the Republic of Austria, the European Anti-Fraud Office and other stakeholders. Its main aim is to reduce the gaps in knowledge and practice in the field of anti-corruption through measures like academic research, cooperation, anti-corruption education and networking.

In 2009, the Global Compact Society in India hosted a workshop on the benefits of greater compliance with the Global Compact's Tenth Principle.

In 2012, the Central Vigilance Commission had been chosen to lead a 10-member global task force and prepare a knowledge management system. It will be a first-of-its-kind which will help in promoting global cooperation in anti-corruption measures.

Transparency International India (TII) is the accredited Indian Chapter of Transparency International; it is an extension of the parent organization with an aim to create a corruption-free India. Its main aim is to promote transparent and ethical governance, and to eliminate corruption. TII has several state chapters so that it can fulfill its mission of eradicating corruption at the grassroots level. TII has also implemented several grassroots initiatives and pacts like the Integrity Pact, Development Pact and Pahal to promote tools of active participation and good governance, and to implement rights-based approaches.

At the Second Interpol Global Programme on Anti Corruption and Asset Recovery held in Delhi in 2012, several top-level Indian officials emphasized the importance of various factors like transparency and accountability in development programmes initiated by government, international cooperation among law enforcement agencies, asset recovery and impounding of proceeds of corruption, and equitable distribution of powers are needed to combat corruption.

India, having met the strict evaluation norms of the Financial Action Task Force (on Money Laundering) (FATF), was granted full-fledged membership in June 2010. The main purpose of FATF is to develop policies to combat money laundering and terrorism financing. This development shows that India is fully committed to following the FATF norms.

The 2011 Indian anti-corruption movement (a series of protests and demonstrations across India) was a major mass movement with an aim to pressurize the Indian Government to bring about a robust legislation and enforcement of laws against corruption.

Some of India's leading companies like Wipro, Genpact, Bajaj Auto and Infosys have joined the ranks of international companies like Siemens and ABB in a global business coalition against corruption through an initiative of the World Economic Forum. This is a proactive corporate step because if businesses can clean up corruption in business to business scenarios, they can succeed in setting the stage to tackle business to government scenarios of corruption as well.

These are the various moves India has taken over the last decade, which go to show that India considers corruption as a war that has to be fought on all fronts. India is prepping itself to get into the top gear for the anti-corruption drive.

8.3 What We can Do—Make the Right Choices

We as concerned citizens of our world need to take our fight against corruption beyond mere flyers, speeches, posters, rallies and slogans. The plague of corruption won't stop spreading unless we pledge to stop it by making the right choices:

A. Choose to influence government agenda to create laws

B. Choose to report cases of corruption

C. Choose to lobby for legislation of anti-corruption reforms

D. Choose to adhere to the code of ethics in all matters

E. Choose to join anti-corruption campaigns and projects

F. Choose to press for accountability

G. Choose to contribute in building a strong civil society

H. Choose to mobilize public action

I. And above all choose not to give or receive bribes

Country-specific anti-corruption organizations need to join hands with the global-level efforts. Several established global organizations like the World Bank, United Nations Office of Drugs and Crime, etc., provide assistance to countries in fighting corruption. For example, the Stolen Asset Recovery (StAR) Initiative launched by the United Nations Office of Drugs and Crime and the World Bank is making significant contribution to the anti-corruption process by recovering stolen assets and preventing laundering acts. A strong partnership between nations and financial centers is needed to implement innovative anti-corruption policy reforms and strategies.

Spotlight

Corruption has to be tackled from the top down and from the bottom up by combining the pressure from above with the voice from below.

The international community needs to formulate a robust framework for increasing awareness of the challenges faced by various international bodies in their anti-corruption efforts and for formulating methods through collective action for overcoming these challenges.

8.3.1 *The International Anti-Corruption Day—More Than a Pledge*

The United Nations General Assembly designated 9th December as the International Anti-Corruption Day. The International Anti-Corruption Day is observed on December 9th each year, since the passage of the United Nations Convention Against Corruption on 31st October 2003. Its main aim is to raise public awareness of corruption and what can be done to fight it, and also to raise awareness of the role of the United Nations Convention Against Corruption. This day is a global observance and not a public holiday.

India needs to really leverage the action points put forth by the UN for this day. India should promote this day and its programs for engaging the masses to effectively fight against corruption. It is a yearly reminder to each one of us to renew our resolve to reduce corruption. Such days have definitely changed our attitude towards corruption. As recently as ten years ago, corruption was only whispered about. Today, people not only talk about corruption but are also campaigning against it.

The Indian subcontinent needs to realize that this day is not meant merely for lobby groups, political leaders and governments, but it is also to be observed and promoted by each and every element of society. By first adopting this day at an individual level, then at an organization level (schools, colleges, companies, etc.) and then finally at the society level, each one of us can then imbibe it as a part of our DNA and strengthen our own commitment to fight corruption. Thereafter, each day will be celebrated as the International Anti-Corruption Day—a pledge to promote this day each and every day—to send out a powerful message that corruption is not at all acceptable.

8.4 Future of Global Efforts—People Power is the Key

Global anti-corruption efforts will continue to be led by leading industrialized nations like the United States and the United Kingdom. But even developing countries like India will inspire other nations to join the bandwagon of anti-corruption.

The way forward is to fight corruption by mobilizing, empowering and connecting people from all sectors and countries. This view was also echoed during the 14th International Anti-Corruption Conference (IACC) in 2010.

The public outcry against corrupt authorities in 2011 and 2012 in India and in the Middle East has set the stage for overthrowing authoritarian regimes.

Eliminating bribery will continue to take center stage in the corporate world. Sector-based enforcements and regulations will be on the rise (for example, banking and finance sectors).

Regular reviews of reforms will become a part of the anti-corruption strategy as they are necessary to weed out systems which are complicated and opaque.

According to the PwC's Confronting Corruption Report (PwC—PricewaterhouseCoopers is the world's largest value-added professional services firm), the business world is more aware than ever of the dangers of corruption, yet the business world will need more stringent controls to deal with corruption risks. From this report, it is evident that in the days to come, the business world will need to gear itself for better anti-corruption measures so that it can lessen the number of real and significant business opportunities lost because of corruption risks. Companies want to have a socially responsible marketplace as a part of the business landscape of the future. Investors and other stakeholders are increasingly keeping a vigilant tab on how their companies handle corporate social responsibility including anti-corruption efforts. There will be an increased focus on the private sector's role in fighting corruption.

As far as India is concerned, it will need to fine-tune its acts and laws. For example, in the case of the Right to Information Act, though it is a big step towards greater accountability and transparency, India will need to overcome criticism and loopholes like the lack of protection for whistleblowers, too many exemptions in the act, etc. Despite the fact that provisions have been made in the Prevention of Corruption Act (this act is a federal law enacted by the Parliament of India to combat corruption in public sector businesses and government agencies in India) to include a larger pool of government employees (government employees, bodies owned or aided or controlled by the government, people working at facilities financed by the government), there are certain loopholes like the lack of provisions for the punishment of foreign perpetrators of corruption, for the penalization of corruption by Indian citizens or corporations in international business transactions, etc. Provisions for overcoming these loopholes need to be introduced in order to bring this act up to par with the international standard of fighting corruption.

Over the past few years, tougher enforcement of anti-corruption laws has become the norm. Laws against bribery and other forms of corruption have become stringent and more global. This trend was seen in 2011 and 2012 and hopefully will continue in the coming years.

For these efforts to work well, the starting point is to fill the gaps in senior international anti-corruption leadership. Contribution in this direction needs to come in from all corners—leaders of nations, national development agencies, law reform commissions, multilateral development banks, the United Nations, Summits like G-20, etc. Only then meaningful progress can be made on the global anti-corruption agenda.

8.5 Final Thoughts—A Deep-Rooted Culture of Anti-Corruption

Anti-corruption agencies and authorities should be aware of the various dimensions of corruption like a thorough understanding of the negative effects of corruption, political, historical and economic context of corruption, dynamics of organized crime, accountability issues, etc.

The use of modern technologies like mobile phones and the Internet through open government initiatives, e-government programs, integrity applications, etc., can help to improve citizen participation, governance, monitoring and transparency.

> **Spotlight**
>
> The key pillars of empowerment and partnership will help nations in not only tackling local acts of corruption, but also acts of internal corruption that have cross-border ramifications.

A critical aspect in winning the fight against corruption is long-term cooperation between all the stakeholders like governments, regulatory authorities, legal tools and institutions, development agencies, financial centers, citizens, civil society, academic communities, human rights defenders, media, local chambers of industry and commerce, donor agencies, NGOs, and public and private sectors. For sustaining this global cooperation, a deep-rooted culture of anti-corruption is the need of the hour. Another key pillar for making global anti-corruption initiatives a worldwide success is empowerment. Empowerment can be achieved when countries share knowledge, training resources, international standards and best practices with each other.

Anti-corruption is everyone's business—finally, we have to adopt the essence of the following sloka (a Sanskrit verse) "Sathyam vada dharmam chara" in order to achieve the vision of a less corrupt and more progressive India. This verse means "Speak truth and lead a righteous life,"—and it is applicable to one and all, irrespective of country, caste, sex, sect, religion, educational qualification and economic status.

So there you have it—how, who, when, why, what and what next of corruption in the world (in general) and in India (in particular).

8.6 Questions for Reflection

A. How global is the scope of anti-bribery laws?

B. What kind of international standards can be established for recovering assets that have been stolen through acts of corruption?

C. Why is the OECD Anti-Bribery Convention important?

D. Is the international anti-corruption agenda based on cultural imperialism?

E. What are the key pillars of global anti-corruption efforts?

F. In what ways can the academic community contribute to the existing monitoring mechanisms?

G. How do the international economic and political power structures affect global-level corruption?

H. In what way has globalization altered the nature of corruption?

Appendices

Appendix A

Useful Resources

Appendix A provides a snapshot of the various learning material and useful resources available for further reading and study. Apart from book details, papers, essays and website links for further reading, study and research, this appendix also shares information about various civil sector initiatives, private bodies and government agencies, which you can be a part of to contribute your share of efforts in the fight against corruption.

Books, White Papers, Journal Reports and Scholarly Articles: The following list contains details of books, white papers, journal reports, essays and scholarly articles for further reading and research related to corruption and its dynamics affecting India and the global landscape.

A. Anne Marie Goetz, Rob Jenkins. 2005. Reinventing Accountability: Making Democracy Work for Human Development. Basingstoke: Palgrave Macmillan.

B. Basu, Kaushik; Bhattacharya, Sudipto; Mishra, Ajit. 1992. "Notes on Bribery and the Control of Corruption." *Journal of Public Economics*, 48 (3): 349-59.

C. Jabbra, J.G. "Bureaucratic Corruption in the Third World: Causes and Remedies." *Indian Journal of Public Administration*, 22:673-91 (October-December 1976).

D. Michael Johnston, 2005, *Syndromes of Corruption: Wealth, Power and Democracy*, Cambridge University Press.

E. Bohara AK, Mitchell NJ, Mittendorff CF (2004). Compound Democracy and the Control of Corruption: A Cross-Country Investigation. *Policy Stud J,* 32(4): 481-99.

F. Mishra, Satish C. 2007. "The Political Economy of Corruption and Economic Growth." Technical background paper commissioned for the Asia Pacific Human Development Report on Corruption. Colombo: UNDP Regional Centre.

G. White paper on Black Money by Indian Ministry of Finance: http://www.thehindubusinessline.com/multimedia/archive/01091/WhitePaper_BackMon_1091518a.pdf

Websites and Links: There are numerous web resources that deal with corruption in India and in the world. The following list is rich in information on various aspects of corruption, right from contexts of corruption and anti-corruption tools to corruption-related data and research.

A. www.u4.no—is a web-based resource centre for donor practitioners and development agencies to effectively address corruption challenges. It maintains resource pages on various themes developed for a donor audience like Corruption in the Health Sector, Political Corruption, etc.

B. http://info.worldbank.org/etools/antic/index.asp—the World Bank Institute—Business Fighting Corruption—an online resource center that provides a "collective action" approach for the business world in fighting corruption by engaging with other companies, governments and civil society in creating a transparent business climate.

C. www.carnegieendowment.org/events/index.cfm?fa=eventDetail&id=49—Florini, Ann. 2000. Transnational Civil Society Networks. Managing Global Issues Project, Carnegie Endowment for International Peace, Washington, DC. 14 March.

D. www.worldbank.org/en/country/india—World Bank: India Data Profile—provides information on news and views, data, research, programs and projects, etc., related to dynamics of corruption and various other factors in India.

E. http://mirror.undp.org/magnet/docs/efa/corruption/Chapter03.pdf—Corruption and Anti-Corruption Strategies: Issues and Case Studies from Developing Countries.

Civil Sector Initiatives, Private Bodies and Government Agencies: There are numerous organizations working relentlessly towards realizing the goal of a corruption-free world. Below is information on some of these organizations.

A. Center for International Private Enterprise (CIPE)—CIPE is one of the four core institutes of the National Endowment for Democracy with an aim to strengthen democracy around the globe through private enterprise and market-oriented reform. It firmly believes in a cross-sector approach of cooperation between governments, civil society and the private sector for addressing the economic, social and political dimensions of corruption effectively.

B. Central Vigilance Commission (CVC)—CVC is an apex Indian governmental body with an aim to advice and guide Central Government agencies in the field of vigilance. It was set up by the Government of India to deal with governmental corruption.

C. Global Infrastructure Anti-Corruption Centre (GIACC)—GIACC is an independent not-for-profit organization that provides resources to assist in the understanding, identification and prevention of corruption in the construction, engineering and infrastructure sectors. It provides online advice and resources on corruption-related aspects, anti-corruption conventions, anti-corruption tools, forums, indices and surveys, etc.

D. India Against Corruption Jan Andolan (IAC)—IAC is a collective organized synergistic People's Movement with an aim to encourage direct participatory democracy of citizens to eliminate corruption from the Indian soil.

E. Transparency International (TI) is a global civil society organization that monitors and publicizes corporate and political corruption in international development and rates countries on a corruption scale. TI is a non-governmental organization that works with partners in government, business and civil society to put effective measures in place to tackle corruption.

F. United Nations Convention Against Corruption (UNCAC)—UNCAC is a major step in promoting international cooperation against corruption. UNCAC is the first globally legally binding international anti-corruption instrument. It is a landmark treaty not only in terms of its wide coverage but also for its provisions and practices like sharing good practices, research, peer reviews, training, etc.

Appendix B

Corruption Studies, Indices and More

Increasing public interest and concern over corruption has led to considerable improvements in the field of design and implementation of surveys and in the construction of composite indices. Appendix B contains information and resources on the corruption studies, indices, diagnostic tools, surveys, expert assessments and reports, which not only give us insights on the corruption scenarios in India, but also deal with various aspects like cross-country analysis, strengths and weaknesses of anti-corruption tools worldwide, overview of corruption-related problems, etc.

A. Global Integrity reports (http://www.globalintegrity.org/report) assess the strengths and weaknesses of anti-corruption mechanisms worldwide, transparency of the public procurement process, media freedom, etc., with an aim to help advocates, policymakers, journalists and citizens to identify and anticipate the areas where corruption is more likely to occur.

B. Central Vigilance Commission Annual Report provides the details of the work carried out by the Central Vigilance Commission and also covers aspects like details of inquiries in scams, system failures and improvements, preventive measures, etc.

C. For quantitative evidence and hard data on Indian corruption, CMS is the key source. The website www.cmsindia.org is a resource hub containing information regarding its activities in the areas of behavioral change, social development, service delivery, transparency in government, etc. CMS believes in bringing about social change, equitable development and responsive governance through research, advocacy, knowledge and capacity building. It has been working on long term partnership as "Research Partner" to UNICEF, Centre for Civil Society, Academy for Educational Development, Transparency India International to name a few.

D. Judicial Reform Network in the 21st Century (JRN21)—JRN21 collects, collates and disseminates documents and papers from meetings and activities on judicial reforms worldwide. JRN21 disseminates knowledge of the best practices and lessons learned in order to bring about independent, accountable and transparent judiciaries.

E. KPMG's Survey on Bribery and Corruption: Impact on Economy and Business Environment 2011—captures the perceptions of Indian corporates of how corruption is corroding the economy as well as the corporate environment: http://www.kpmg.com/IN/en/IssuesAndInsights/ThoughtLeadership/KPMG_Bribery_Survey_Report_new.pdf

F. Transparency International's Corruption Perceptions Index (CPI) captures the informed views of analysts, business people and experts in countries around the world through surveys and assessments in order to measure the perceived levels of public sector corruption.

G. The World Bank Institute (www.worldbank.org/wbi) and the World Bank (www.worldbank.org) websites contain information on various aspects related to corruption, right from diagnostic tools to survey results.

H. World Bank Control of Corruption Index (CCI)—CCI is an aggregation of various indicators that measure the degree to which corruption is perceived to exist among public officials, businesses and politicians. CCI measures the extent to which public power is exercised for private gain, including both petty and grand forms of corruption, as well as "capture" of the state by elites and private interests.

References

1. Andvig, J., and K.O. Moene. 1990. "How Corruption May Corrupt." *Journal of Economic Behaviour and Organization,* 3 (1): 63-76.
2. Carl J. Friedrich. "Corruption Concepts in Historical Perspective," in Arnold J. Heidenheimer, Michael Johnston and Victor T. LeVine, eds. *Political Corruption: A Handbook* (New Brunswick: Transaction Publishers, 1989), p. 15. Also, Friedrich, *The Pathology of Politics: Violence, Betrayal, Corruption, Secrecy and Propaganda* (New York: Harper & Row, 1972), pp. 127-41.
3. Mauro, P. 1995. "Corruption and Growth", *Quarterly Journal of Economics*, 110(3), 681-712.
4. PwC's Confronting Corruption Report: http://www.pwc.com/gx/en/forensic-accounting-dispute-consulting-services/pdf/pwc-confronting-corruption.pdf
5. Report of the Central Vigilance Commission. 1966 (New Delhi: Government of India, 1966), pp. 15-16 and 32-33.
6. "Report of the SEBI Committee on Corporate Governance, February 2003". SEBI Committee on Corporate Governance. http://www.sebi.gov.in/commreport/corpgov.pdf
7. Transparency International Corruption Report: http://www.transparency.org/policy_research/surveys_indices/cpi/ 2005
8. World Bank. 2006. "Guidelines: Procurement under IBRD Loans and IDA Credits" (Washington, DC: World Bank).